An Inspector Calls

A Complete Revision Guide for Edexcel IGCSE English Literature

Essential Literature: Complete Edexcel IGCSE Revision Series

Colour My Learning

BAILBROOK LANE

Contents

Foreword	vii
1. INTRODUCTION	**1**
Purpose of This Guide	1
How to Use This Revision Guide	1
What's Inside and When to Use It:	2
Overview of the Exam Format (Edexcel IGCSE – Paper 2, 4ET1/02)	3
2. STORY OVERVIEW	**5**
Plot Summary	5
Brief Act-by-act summaries	6
Detailed Act-by-Act Breakdown	8
Self-Test: Story Overview	10
3. MAIN CHARACTERS	**12**
Full Character List – *An Inspector Calls*	13
Detailed character profiles	14
Self-Test: Main Characters	35
4. CONTEXTUAL BACKGROUND	**38**
Author Background and Purpose	39
Historical, Social, and Political Context	40
Thematic Relevance of Context	41
Structural and Symbolic Elements Supporting Context	42
Self-Test: Contextual Background	43
5. MAIN THEMES AND KEY QUOTES	**46**
Social Responsibility	47
Class and Social Hierarchy	50
Generational Conflict	52
Gender and Power	55
Power and Authority	57
Truth, Illusion, and Deception	60

Change and Redemption	62
How to Write About Themes in An Inspector Calls	65
Self-Test: Main Themes and Key Quotes	67

6. **GLOSSARY OF KEY LITERARY AND DRAMATIC TERMS** — 71

Language Techniques	71
Structure and Plot	73
Dramatic Form and Devices	74
Literary Concepts and Critical Terms	75
Using This Glossary as You Write	76
Self-test: Glossary of Literary and Dramatic Terms	77

7. **LANGUAGE, FORM AND STRUCTURE** — 79

How to Use This Section	79
Language	80
Form	84
Structure	88
AO2 Starter Pack – Good Techniques to Learn First	93
Self-test: Language, Form and Structure	94

8. **HOW TO WRITE YOUR ESSAYS** — 95

Using a Structure to Plan and Write Effective Essays	95
Sample Essay Plans	100
Skeleton Structures for Essay Responses	102
Why Use This Structure	104
Planning Templates	104

9. **QUICK RECAP TOOLS** — 107

Revision Checklist	107

10. **PRACTICE EXAM QUESTIONS** — 111

Observed Trends	112
Revision Tips	112
Social Responsibility	112
Class and Social Hierarchy	113

Generational Conflict	114
Gender and Power	114
Power and Authority	115
Truth, Illusion and Deception	115
Justice and Consequence	116
Change and Redemption	116
Dramatic Form and Structure	116
Symbolism and Interpretation	117
Download: *An Inspector Calls* – Past Exam Questions by Theme (Ebook)	118
11. FURTHER READING AND RESOURCES	**119**
ColourMyLearning	120
BBC Bitesize – An Inspector Calls (GCSE English Literature)	120
Edexcel Examiner Reports – English Literature Paper 2	121
ANSWER KEY	122
Chapter 2 Story Overview	122
Chapter 3 Main Characters	123
Chapter 4 Context	126
Chapter 5 Main Themes and Key Quotes	128
Chapter 6 Glossary of Literary and Dramatic Terms	132
Chapter 7 Language Form and Structure	133
Chapter 9 Quick Recap Tools	135
Acknowledgments	137
Also by Colour My Learning	139

Written by Colour My Learning

© 2025 Xelium Ltd. All rights reserved.

Published by **Bailbrook Lane**, an imprint of Xelium Ltd.

Created in collaboration with **Colour My Learning**, a Xelium Ltd brand.

This product is for **personal educational use only** and may not be copied, redistributed, or modified without permission.

No part of this publication may be reproduced, stored in a retrieval system, or transmitted in any form or by any means electronic, mechanical, photocopying, recording, or otherwise without the prior written permission of the publisher, except in the case of brief quotations used for review or educational purposes. For licensing or permission enquiries, contact:

Bailbrook Lane info@bailbrooklane.com | www.bailbrooklane.com

In collaboration with: Colour My Learning www.colourmylearning.com

Updated Oct 2025 Edition – includes minor updates to terminology and analysis in the *Language, Form and Structure* section, aligned with Edexcel guidance on dramatic texts.

Cover design by Samuel JA Tan
eBook ISBN 978-1-913557-50-8
Paperback ISBN 978-1-913557-51-5

Foreword

Welcome to this *An Inspector Calls* revision guide, written to support you as you work towards exam success and a deeper understanding of the play.

This guide is designed to complement—rather than replace—the teaching and guidance you receive from your teacher. Use it as a companion: to consolidate your learning, sharpen your analysis, and prepare effectively for your English Literature exam.

Every effort has been made to ensure the content is accurate, useful, and aligned with the Edexcel IGCSE specification. If you notice any errors or have suggestions for improvement, we would be grateful to hear from you. Your feedback helps us make future editions even better.

If you find this guide helpful, we'd love to hear from you. You can leave a review on: Amazon or Bailbrook Lane

We wish you every success in your studies. Read critically,

Foreword

revise actively and write with clarity and purpose. Good luck in your exams!

With best wishes,

The team at **Colour My Learning**

and **Bailbrook Lane**

Chapter 1
Introduction

Purpose of This Guide

This guide is designed to help you if you are studying *An Inspector Calls* for the Edexcel International GCSE in English Literature prepare effectively for the exam. It focuses on helping you:

- understand key characters, themes, and context
- analyse language, structure and form
- practise applying their knowledge to exam-style questions

How to Use This Revision Guide

This guide is designed to support your study of *An Inspector Calls* **after you've completed your first reading of the play** — whether in class or independently. It provides a clear structure to help you revise plot, explore themes, understand characters, and prepare effectively for your exam.

Use it as a complete revision tool or return to specific sections as needed.

What's Inside and When to Use It:

1. **Start with the Story Overview** Begin by revisiting the plot summary and key turning points. This helps you anchor your understanding of what happens — and why it matters.
2. **Study the Characters and Themes Together** Each theme is explored alongside key character contributions and carefully selected quotes with analysis. This combined approach helps you understand how Priestley uses character to communicate ideas and build meaning.
3. **Revisit Language, Form and Structure** This section helps you meet AO2 by explaining how the play is constructed and how specific techniques affect the audience. Use the model paragraphs as a reference when planning your own essays.
4. **Apply What You've Learned** You'll find past paper questions, short tasks, and planning prompts that allow you to put your knowledge into practice. Use these for timed practice, homework, or in-class activities.
5. **Review Key Quotes and Ideas** Quick-recap tools and quote summaries are included throughout, so you can revise efficiently and reinforce what you've learned.

This guide can be used alongside classroom teaching or for independent revision. Whether you're working steadily across the term or reviewing ahead of your exams, it offers structured support to help you write clearly, revise with focus, and understand the play with confidence.

Overview of the Exam Format (Edexcel IGCSE – Paper 2, 4ET1/02)

Section A: Modern Drama

This section accounts for 20% of the total English Literature Qualification.

- 1 hour 30 minutes total paper (including Section B: Literary Heritage)
- Choose 1 out of 2 questions on *An Inspector Calls*
- 30 marks | Spend approx. 45 minutes
- Open book: You may take a clean copy of the play into the exam

You are expected to

- demonstrate a close understanding of their drama text
- maintain a critical style
- present an informed personal engagement
- understand how writers create literary effects
- understand and use appropriate literary terminology
- identify and use relevant examples from the play.

An Inspector Calls

Assessment Objectives Tested:

AO1: Understanding of the text and personal engagement (15 marks)

AO2: Analysis of language, form, and structure (15 marks)

Chapter 2
Story Overview

Plot Summary

Set in 1912, *An Inspector Calls* is a morality play written by J.B. Priestley in 1945. The action unfolds in real time over a single evening, in the dining room of the affluent Birling family in Brumley, a fictional industrial city.

The Birlings are celebrating the engagement of their daughter Sheila to Gerald Croft. Their celebration is interrupted by the unexpected arrival of Inspector Goole, who is investigating the suicide of a young working-class woman named Eva Smith.

Through his interrogation, the Inspector gradually reveals that each member of the family — and Gerald — played a role in Eva's downfall. As their secrets unravel, the play critiques social inequality, moral responsibility, and the illusion of respectability.

The play ends with a twist: after the Inspector departs and the family begins to rationalise their actions, they receive a phone call informing them that a real inspector is on his way to investigate the suicide of a young woman — suggesting a second chance to learn their lesson or face consequences.

🖊 Extension Task: Write a short review of how the play would change if set in a modern context (e.g. 2025). What events, attitudes, or symbols might need to change?

Brief Act-by-act summaries

Act 1:

- The Birlings are dining and celebrating Sheila and Gerald's engagement.
- Mr Birling makes self-important speeches about business, war (wrongly predicting peace), and individualism.
- Inspector Goole arrives, announcing the suicide of Eva Smith.
- Mr Birling admits he sacked Eva from his factory. Sheila recognises Eva as someone she had fired out of jealousy from a department store.
- The tension begins to rise as the Inspector's moral probing deepens.

🖊 Discuss: Why do you think Priestley chose to begin the play during a celebration? What impact does this have on the audience's expectations?

Act 2:

- Gerald confesses to an affair with Eva (then called Daisy Renton).
- Sheila becomes more self-aware and supportive of the Inspector's message.
- Mrs Birling, head of a charity, denies Eva help and shows no remorse — unaware that Eva was pregnant.
- The Inspector corners Mrs Birling, who insists the father of Eva's child should take full responsibility — only to learn that the father is her son, Eric.

Act 3:

- Eric confesses to a drunken encounter with Eva that led to her pregnancy and his theft of money to support her.
- The Inspector delivers a powerful speech on collective responsibility: "We are members of one body."
- After the Inspector leaves, the family debates whether he was real.
- A call to the local police confirms there is no Inspector Goole.
- Just as they begin to relax, the phone rings again — a girl has just died, and a police inspector is on his way.

For additional practice and understanding the plot better

AO1: In two sentences, explain how the three-act structure builds tension before the Inspector arrives.

AO2: Identify one structural device (refer Chapter 7 Language, Form and Structure) in Act 2 that heightens moral conflict—and say how it does so.

Detailed Act-by-Act Breakdown

Act 1 – Setting the Stage and Early Revelations

Scene 1: The Celebration

The play opens in the Birling's dining room during a dinner party to celebrate Sheila Birling's engagement to Gerald Croft. The mood is light, smug, and self-congratulatory. Mr Birling gives pompous speeches about individual responsibility and the impossibility of war or social upheaval.

Key line: "A man has to mind his own business."

Scene 2: The Inspector Arrives

Inspector Goole arrives unexpectedly, announcing that a young woman, Eva Smith, has committed suicide. He begins questioning Mr Birling, who admits to sacking Eva from his factory for leading a strike. Sheila is next — she had Eva dismissed from Milwards out of jealousy and admits her guilt. Gerald is visibly shaken when Eva's new name, Daisy Renton, is mentioned. Tension builds, and the family starts to feel the Inspector's moral pressure.

✏️ Reflection Prompt: How does the arrival of the Inspector shift the tone of the play? What do you think the audience is meant to start questioning at this point?

Act 2 – Deeper Exposure and Moral Conflict

Scene 3: Gerald's Confession

Gerald reveals he had an affair with Daisy Renton the previous summer but broke it off. He helped her during a difficult time, but also used her. Sheila returns Gerald's engagement ring and criticises his lack of honesty.

Scene 4: Mrs Birling's Interrogation

Mrs Sybil Birling, proud and cold, refuses to take any responsibility. She describes rejecting Eva's plea for help from her charity because Eva used the name "Mrs Birling". She insists the father of the unborn child is to blame and should face consequences — unaware that it's Eric.

✏ Extension Task: Write a 100-word diary entry from Eva's perspective after being turned away by Mrs Birling. Focus on her emotional state and use implied tone.

Act 3 – Climax, Collapse and Consequences

Scene 5: Eric's Confession

Eric enters and admits he drunkenly forced himself on Eva, got her pregnant, and tried to support her with stolen money. The family is in disarray. The Inspector condemns them all and delivers his famous final speech:

"We don't live alone. We are members of one body. We are responsible for each other."

Scene 6: Doubt and Denial

After the Inspector leaves, the Birlings question his identity.

They begin to convince themselves it was a hoax: there is no Inspector Goole at the police station and no recent suicide.

Scene 7: The Final Twist

Just as Mr Birling is gloating about a close escape, the phone rings. A young woman has just died and a real Police Inspector is on his way to question them.

✏️ Reflection: What emotion do you think Priestley wanted the audience to feel at the end of the play? How effective is the twist in delivering this?

Self-Test: Story Overview

Use the following questions to check your understanding. No peeking — test yourself from memory first.

Multiple Choice:

1. Where is *An Inspector Calls* set?
    a. London
    b. Brumley
    c. Manchester
    d. Birmingham
2. When is the play set?
    a. 1945
    b. 1939
    c. 1912
    d. 1925

Short Answer:

3. What is Mr Birling's reason for sacking Eva Smith?
4. Why does Sheila feel responsible for Eva's dismissal from Milwards?
5. What dramatic device is used at the very end of the play to surprise the audience?

Write Brief Notes:

6. Write 3-4 bullet points summarising Gerald's involvement with Eva Smith/Daisy Renton.
7. What are two key ways the Inspector challenges the Birlings' worldview?

Chapter 3
Main Characters

In *An Inspector Calls*, J.B. Priestley crafts a tightly focused cast of characters, each representing a different segment of Edwardian society and a distinct moral position. The interactions between these characters drive the narrative and bring Priestley's central messages to life.

This section explores the major and symbolic roles each character plays within the plot. You'll find:

- full list of characters
- detailed profiles that reveal key traits and motivations
- how each character changes (or refuses to)
- their involvement in Eva Smith's downfall
- links to major themes and social ideas
- key moments and quotes to support exam responses

Understanding these characters in depth is crucial to mastering AO1 and AO2 — demonstrating knowledge of the text and analysing how Priestley uses them to shape meaning.

Think not just about *what* they do, but *why*, and *what Priestley wants us to learn from them.*

Full Character List – *An Inspector Calls*

Main Characters

1. **Arthur Birling** – A wealthy businessman and father
2. **Sybil Birling** – His wife, involved in charitable work
3. **Sheila Birling** – Their daughter, engaged to Gerald
4. **Eric Birling** – Their son, troubled and secretive
5. **Gerald Croft** – Sheila's fiancé, from another wealthy family
6. **Inspector Goole** – The mysterious inspector investigating Eva Smith's death

Significant Offstage Characters

1. **Eva Smith / Daisy Renton** – The young woman who dies by suicide, never appears on stage but is central to the plot

Minor / Mentioned Characters

1. **Edna** – The Birlings' maid; silent presence, represents the working class and class divisions within the household
2. **Alderman Meggarty** – Mentioned by Gerald; a supposedly respectable figure who sexually harasses women

3. **The Inspector (real)** – Referenced in the twist ending, suggesting a real police inspector is about to call
4. **The Palace Bar owner and staff** – Gerald refers to this setting during his account of meeting Daisy Renton

✏️ Quick Recap: Group the characters into three categories: Main, Offstage, and Minor. Write one sentence on why each group is important to the play's structure.

Detailed character profiles

Mr Arthur Birling

Role in Plot:

Arthur Birling is the patriarch of the Birling family and a self-made businessman. He **represents the capitalist elite** and is used by Priestley to **symbolise complacency and arrogance among the upper classes**. He is the dramatic foil of the Inspector.

Key Traits:

Arrogant, pompous, self-serving, dismissive of social responsibility, optimistic to a fault about economics and politics.

Motivations:

Protecting his social standing, securing a business alliance through Sheila's engagement to Gerald, and avoiding scandal at all costs.

Character Development:

He experiences no genuine development or remorse. He remains obsessed with status and dismissive of the Inspector's message, even at the end of the play.

Symbolism:

Represents capitalism, patriarchy, and outdated Edwardian values. He is the mouthpiece for anti-socialist ideals and industrial selfishness.

Themes Linked:

Social Responsibility, Class and Social Hierarchy, Power and Authority, Generational Conflict, Appearance vs Reality

Key Moments / Turning Points:

- His confident, ironic speeches about the impossibility of war and the Titanic sinking.
- His justification for sacking Eva Smith: "If you don't come down sharply on these people, they'd soon be asking for the earth."
- His reaction after the Inspector leaves, focusing on a potential scandal more than moral responsibility.

Conflicts & Interactions:

- Defends capitalism and opposes the Inspector's ideas.
- Dismisses the concerns of Sheila and Eric, revealing the generational divide.
- Often clashes with Inspector Goole and is undermined by his own hypocrisy.

Quotes (with Analysis):

"The way some of these cranks talk and write now, you'd think everybody has to look after everybody else."
Shows his disdain for socialist thinking and foreshadows his rejection of responsibility.

"The Titanic... unsinkable, absolutely unsinkable."
A moment of dramatic irony; the audience knows he's wrong, which undermines his authority and judgement.

"A man has to mind his own business and look after himself and his own."
Reflects his individualist ideology — a direct contrast to the Inspector's communal message.

"If you don't come down sharply on these people, they'd soon be asking for the earth."
Reveals his fear of social uprising and lack of empathy towards workers.

"Community and all that nonsense….mixed up together like bees in a hive."
Dismisses collective values; shows his rejection of social responsibility and mockery of progressive ideas.

"A man has to mind his own business and look after himself and his own"
Justifies his behaviour and actions in order to support his capitalist desires

"There's every excuse for what your mother and I did."
Defends their actions without remorse, showing concern only for damage control.

🖊 Extension Task: Write a short speech from Arthur Birling's perspective defending his actions. Then, write a rebuttal as if spoken by the Inspector.

🖊 Discuss: Which of Arthur Birling's beliefs do you think Priestley criticises most — and why? Discuss with a partner.

Mrs Sybil Birling

Role in Plot:

Sybil Birling is the matriarch of the family and chair of a local women's charity. She **represents upper-class hypocrisy, moral coldness, and a rigid adherence to social hierarchy**. Her interrogation reveals deep class prejudice and an utter lack of empathy.

Key Traits:

Proud, cold, snobbish, morally rigid, emotionally detached, class-conscious.

Motivations:

Maintaining family reputation, defending her social class, and upholding traditional values. She believes firmly in the idea of social superiority and moral purity — especially among the upper classes.

Character Development:

Sybil does not change throughout the play. Even when confronted with her actions' consequences, she refuses to accept blame or learn from the Inspector's message. Her character is a symbol of entrenched, unrepentant privilege.

Symbolism:

Represents the aristocratic mindset of the Edwardian upper class — emotionally and morally disconnected from the lower classes. She also embodies the failure of charitable institutions when they are influenced by personal bias.

Themes Linked:

Social Responsibility, Class and Social Hierarchy, Gender and Inequality, Appearance vs Reality, Power and Authority

Key Moments / Turning Points:

- Denies Eva help at her charity because she was "impertinent" and used the Birling name.
- Refuses to believe her son Eric could be involved, yet condemns "the father" of Eva's child before knowing it is him.
- Dismisses the Inspector's authority and remains focused on her own innocence.

Conflicts & Interactions:

- Clashes with the Inspector, showing no remorse or self-reflection.
- Has a strained relationship with Sheila, who challenges her mother's lack of empathy.

- Ironically condemns Eric unknowingly, creating dramatic irony.

Quotes (with Analysis):

"I did nothing I'm ashamed of."
Reflects her absolute denial of guilt and emotional disconnection. Priestley uses this to critique the moral failings of the privileged.

"Girls of that class—"
A sharp, revealing moment of class prejudice. Her disdain for the working class is clear and damning.

"As if a girl of that sort would ever refuse money!"
Shows not only classism but also a lack of imagination or compassion for Eva's dignity.

"Go and look for the father of the child. It's his responsibility."
Ironic line that condemns her own son without realising it; exposes her hypocrisy and selective judgement.

"I don't believe it. I won't believe it."
Maintains her moral high ground as she maintains their innocence (and chosen ignorance) in the affair

🖊 Reflection Prompt: What does Sybil Birling's attitude toward Eva reveal about charity, class, and morality in the play?

🖊 Quick Recap: Describe Sybil in 5 words. Then write a one-sentence summary of her moral stance.

An Inspector Calls

Sheila Birling

Role in Plot:

Sheila is Arthur and Sybil Birling's daughter and is initially portrayed as naïve and sheltered. However, she undergoes the most significant transformation in the play, becoming increasingly self-aware, morally conscious, and aligned with the Inspector's message. She serves as Priestley's **symbol of hope and change in the younger generation**.

Key Traits:

Intelligent, emotional, empathetic, idealistic, perceptive, assertive (as she develops).

Motivations:

Initially driven by status and approval, but later becomes motivated by guilt, justice, and the desire to see her family take responsibility for their actions.

Character Development:

Sheila starts as immature and superficial but rapidly evolves into a self-critical, socially aware young woman. She accepts full responsibility for her actions and challenges the hypocrisy of her parents and fiancé. She refuses to return to the illusion of innocence.

Symbolism:

Sheila symbolises the **potential for societal change**, particularly in the post-war generation. She reflects the impact of education, conscience, and progressive values in contrast to her parents' conservative views.

Themes Linked:

Generational Conflict, Social Responsibility, Gender and Inequality, Change and Redemption, Power and Authority

Key Moments / Turning Points:

- Her confession of having Eva sacked from Milwards due to jealousy and vanity.
- Breaking off her engagement with Gerald after learning of his affair — a rejection of superficial appearances and dependency.
- Defending the Inspector's message and condemning her parents' refusal to change.

Conflicts & Interactions:

- Clashes with her parents' denial and complacency.
- Challenges Gerald on honesty and morality.
- Echoes the Inspector's message and even takes on a role similar to his in holding others accountable after he leaves.

Quotes (with Analysis):

"Oh – Gerald – you've got it – is it the one you wanted me to have? ... Look mummy, isn't a beauty!"
Portrays Sheila early on as childish/child-like and materialistic making her character development throughout the play stark and contrasting especially when compared to her parents

An Inspector Calls

"But these girls aren't cheap labour – they're people."
Early sign of her developing conscience and empathy; a clear rejection of her father's capitalist attitude.

"I know I'm to blame – and I'm desperately sorry."
Sheila is one of the few to fully accept responsibility, showing emotional maturity and growth.

"You're beginning to pretend now that nothing's really happened at all."
Condemns her parents' return to denial; shows moral clarity and frustration at their evasiveness.

"I suppose we're all nice people now."
A sarcastic observation that criticises the family's eagerness to forget the Inspector's message.

"It frightens me the way you talk."
Sheila's reaction to her parents' lack of remorse; shows her emotional maturity and rejection of their values.

"It's you two who are being childish – trying not to face the facts."
Pointed revelation of how Sheila's principles have changed while her parents hold on to their beliefs

✏️ Extension Task: Imagine Sheila writes a letter to Eva Smith after the Inspector leaves. What would she say?

✏️ Discuss: Do you think Sheila really changes by the end of the play, or is it temporary? What evidence supports your view?

Eric Birling

Role in Plot:

Eric is the Birlings' troubled and misunderstood son. Although his immaturity and recklessness contribute significantly to Eva Smith's suffering, he ultimately demonstrates remorse and a desire to change. He represents the emotional and moral potential of the younger generation — flawed but capable of learning.

Key Traits:

Awkward, insecure, emotional, impulsive, remorseful, morally conflicted

Motivations:

Initially seeks escape through drinking and rebellion. Later, driven by guilt, he becomes a voice of conscience alongside Sheila, calling for accountability and truth.

Character Development:

Eric transforms from a secretive, reckless young man to someone who acknowledges his wrongdoing and the importance of social responsibility. His breakdown and confession are raw and emotionally charged, setting him apart from the cold rationality of his parents.

Symbolism:

Eric symbolises the **moral awakening of youth**, but also the dangers of privilege without guidance. His storyline critiques male entitlement, class arrogance, and the failure of traditional family values.

An Inspector Calls

Themes Linked:

Generational Conflict, Guilt and Responsibility, Gender and Power, Change and Redemption, Class and Social Hierarchy

Key Moments / Turning Points:

- His nervous behaviour throughout the play hints at deeper involvement.
- His confession of stealing money to support Eva reveals guilt and desperation.
- He breaks emotionally when his mother unknowingly condemns him.
- He condemns both his parents: "You killed her. She came to you to protect me — and you turned her away."

Conflicts & Interactions:

- Clashes repeatedly with Mr Birling, whom he sees as a hypocrite.
- Criticises Mrs Birling for her harshness and lack of maternal instinct.
- His bond with Sheila strengthens as both align morally with the Inspector.

Quotes (with Analysis):

"You're not the kind of father a chap could go to when he's in trouble."
Highlights the emotional neglect in the Birling family and critiques patriarchal authority.

"Why shouldn't they try for higher wages? We try for the highest possible prices."
Eric recognises that workers should be allowed to push for more money in the same way that Mr Birling tries to maximise profit.

I was in that state when a chap easily turns nasty.
An excuse or a euphemism for his regrettable actions (rape) which shows some remorse but still does not amount to owning responsibility for his behaviour.

"We all helped to kill her."
A pivotal admission. Eric fully accepts collective responsibility, unlike his parents.

"My God – I'm not likely to forget."
A raw moment of regret that signals deep emotional impact and long-term change.

"She wouldn't take any more money from me."
Eva maintains her dignity despite desperation; Eric recognises and respects this, deepening his sense of guilt.

🖊 Reflection Prompt: Eric says, "We all helped to kill her." Why is this line so important?

🖊 Quick Recap: List three reasons why Eric's confession is a turning point in the play.

Gerald Croft

Role in Plot:

Gerald is Sheila's fiancé and the son of a wealthy industrialist. He initially appears charming and respectable but is later revealed to have had an affair with Eva/Daisy. He serves as a bridge between the older and younger generations — sympathetic at times, yet unwilling to change fundamentally.

Key Traits:

Confident, composed, socially adept, evasive, morally ambiguous, self-justifying

Motivations:

Preserving his reputation, maintaining social alliances (including his engagement), and avoiding public scandal. While he may have cared for Eva/Daisy, he ultimately prioritises self-preservation.

Character Development:

Gerald experiences temporary discomfort and guilt, especially when confessing his affair. However, by the end of the play, he is quick to accept the idea that the Inspector might be a fake and encourages the others to move on, revealing a lack of true moral growth.

Symbolism:

Gerald represents the **entrenched privilege of the upper class**, and the illusion of decency often upheld by social status. He also reflects the limitations of partial reform — he has empathy but not accountability.

Themes Linked:

Gender and Power, Social Responsibility, Appearance vs Reality, Class Privilege, Moral Ambiguity

Key Moments / Turning Points:

- Confesses to helping Eva/Daisy and housing her, but also admits to a sexual relationship.
- Shows real emotion and nostalgia for his time with her, but distances himself morally.
- Investigates the Inspector's identity, keen to disprove the situation rather than reflect on it.
- Tries to offer Sheila the engagement ring again, assuming everything has returned to normal.

Conflicts & Interactions:

- Affectionate but patronising toward Sheila; fails to understand her growth.
- At odds with the Inspector's probing, though less combative than Mr Birling.
- Attempts to unify the family once doubts arise about the Inspector's authenticity.

Quotes (with Analysis):

"She was young and pretty and warm-hearted – and intensely grateful."
Shows that Gerald was emotionally affected by Eva, but also reflects an imbalanced power dynamic.

"Everything's all right now, Sheila. What about this ring?"
Reveals his failure to grasp the emotional and moral transformation Sheila has undergone.

"We can keep it from the Sheriff. It's bound to be unpleasant and disturbing."
Prioritises reputation over justice; exposes his instinct to cover things up.

I'm rather more – upset – by this business than I probably appear to be –
Suggests Gerald is managing appearances; his remorse may be performative.

It may have all been nonsense
Reflects his move towards self-preservation once the threat to his reputation (the Inspector's credibility) fades.

🖉 Extension Task: Write Gerald's diary entry from the night he confesses his affair. What is he thinking about — Eva, Sheila, or his reputation?

Inspector Goole

Role in Plot:

The Inspector is the play's central catalyst — interrogating the Birlings, revealing their social failings, and delivering Priestley's core messages. His identity remains ambiguous, but his **moral authority** is absolute. He is the vehicle through which Priestley **critiques capitalism and promotes social responsibility**.

Key Traits:

Authoritative, enigmatic, composed, prophetic, moralistic, relentless

Motivations:

Not interested in legal justice, but in moral responsibility. His aim is to force each character — and the audience — to confront the consequences of selfishness, inequality, and lack of compassion.

Character Development:

The Inspector doesn't change — instead, he provokes change (or resistance) in others. His steady presence contrasts sharply with the rising emotional tension he incites.

Symbolism:

Inspector Goole is a **symbol of collective conscience**, justice, and social awareness. He may represent a supernatural or moral force — his name "Goole" echoes "ghoul," suggesting he could be more than human. He embodies Priestley's socialist ideals and ethical urgency.

An Inspector Calls

Themes Linked:

Social Responsibility, Class and Social Hierarchy, Power and Authority, Truth vs Illusion, Change and Redemption

Key Moments / Turning Points:

- Arrives just as Mr Birling preaches individualism and dismisses social duty.
- Guides each character's confession, using calm persistence.
- Delivers the play's most famous speech on collective responsibility.
- Disappears just before the twist — reinforcing his mysterious nature.

Conflicts & Interactions:

- Exposes the hypocrisy of the Birlings, especially Mr and Mrs Birling.
- Earns the respect of Sheila and Eric, who begin to adopt his moral stance.
- Challenges Gerald's shallow repentance and symbolic gestures of reassurance.

Quotes (with Analysis):

"We are members of one body. We are responsible for each other."
Summarises Priestley's core message of collective responsibility. Delivered as a moral statement, not a suggestion.

"Each of you helped to kill her."
Accuses each character directly, forcing acknowledgement of shared guilt and moral failure.

"Public men, Mr Birling, have responsibilities as well as privileges."
Challenges Mr Birling's belief in privilege without accountability; reinforces Priestley's critique of social inequality.

"There are millions and millions of Eva Smiths and John Smiths still left with us."
Expands the play's relevance beyond the Birling family, pointing to the ongoing presence of injustice in society.

"It's better to ask for the earth than to take it."
Suggests that the working class are judged harshly for basic requests, while the powerful take far more without question.

"We don't live alone. We are members of one body."
Repeats the theme of social unity; underscores the Inspector's role as the play's moral voice.

"If men will not learn that lesson, they will be taught it in blood and fire and anguish."
A powerful warning from the Inspector; the biblical and violent imagery reinforces the consequences of ignoring social responsibility.

✏️ Reflection Prompt: The Inspector doesn't change — but he changes everyone else. What does this say about his role in the play?

Eva Smith / Daisy Renton

Role in Plot:

Eva Smith never appears on stage, yet she is the most powerful figure in the play. Her life and death act as the moral test for each character. Through their recollections, we piece together her story — a working-class woman continually failed by the institutions and individuals around her. She is a narrative device and symbolic figure representing the marginalised.

Key Traits:

Industrious, dignified, vulnerable, principled, resilient — though seen only through others' accounts

Motivations:

Survival, dignity, fairness, and independence. Despite facing hardship, Eva maintains a sense of moral integrity, refusing stolen money and appealing for help through proper channels.

Character Development:

Since she never speaks directly, her "development" is revealed retrospectively through increasingly tragic details. She transitions from a hopeful factory worker to a destitute, pregnant woman who takes her own life — a victim of cumulative neglect and exploitation.

Symbolism:

Eva Smith symbolises the **voiceless poor**, particularly working-class women, and the consequences of a society without compassion. She also represents the idea of collective human experience — a single name for millions who suffer unnoticed. The Inspector's final warning that "millions and millions of Eva Smiths and John Smiths" exist reinforces this.

Themes Linked:

Social Responsibility, Class and Social Hierarchy, Gender and Inequality, Power and Exploitation, Appearance vs Reality

Key Moments / Turning Points:

- Sacked by Mr Birling for striking.
- Fired by Sheila due to a petty act of jealousy.
- Kept and discarded by Gerald as a mistress.
- Refused help by Mrs Birling when pregnant and desperate.
- Abused and abandoned by Eric, despite his later remorse.

Conflicts & Interactions:

- Each character's moral failure is revealed through their interaction with her.
- Never speaks — she is a blank canvas for the audience's empathy and the family's guilt.

Quotes (with Analysis):

(Note: All quotes about Eva come from others. These reveal more about the speakers than Eva herself.)

"A girl of that class." – Mrs Birling
Shows disdain and prejudice — Eva is judged by status, not character.

"She had a lot to say – far too much – so she had to go." – Mr Birling
Highlights her independence and the systemic suppression of working-class voices.

"Just used her... as if she was an animal, a thing, not a person." – Inspector Goole
Summarises how the upper class dehumanised her, and what the play condemns.

"She wouldn't take any more money from me." – Eric
Eva's refusal shows integrity and pride; despite her situation, she won't accept stolen money, elevating her moral position.

"She kept a rough sort of diary." – Inspector Goole
Suggests Eva had a voice and perspective of her own, even if it's never directly heard on stage; builds empathy and tragedy.

🖊 Quick Recap: How does Eva's silence make her story more powerful? List two effects of her being offstage throughout the play.

🖊 Extension Task: Write a short monologue that Eva might have delivered if she had appeared on stage. Keep it to one paragraph.

Self-Test: Main Characters

Multiple Choice Questions

Choose the best answer for each question.

1. Which character is most closely associated with Priestley's theme of moral hope and social change?
   a. Mr Birling
   b. Gerald Croft
   c. Sheila Birling
   d. Sybil Birling
2. Who says, "We are members of one body. We are responsible for each other"?
   a. Eric Birling
   b. Inspector Goole
   c. Mr Birling
   d. Eva Smith
3. Why is Eva Smith considered a powerful character despite never appearing on stage?
   a. She is the Inspector's assistant
   b. Her actions drive the Inspector's interrogation
   c. She is a symbolic figure who reveals others' moral failings
   d. She sends letters that guide the plot

An Inspector Calls

4. Which quote best reflects Mr Birling's capitalist ideology?
   a. "Everything's all right now, Sheila."
   b. "If you don't come down sharply on these people…"
   c. "Each of you helped to kill her."
   d. "Public men… have responsibilities as well as privileges."

Short Answer Questions

Write 1–2 sentence responses.

5. What key change occurs in Sheila Birling's character during the play?
6. How does Eric's behaviour contrast with that of his parents by the end of the play?
7. What does Sybil Birling's reaction to Eva's appeal at the charity reveal about her values?
8. In what way does Gerald Croft represent both sympathy and moral failure?

Longer Tasks

Character & Theme Connection

9. Choose one main character. Explain how Priestley uses that character to explore the theme of Social Responsibility. Include:
   - A brief summary of the character's role
   - At least one quotation
   - A comment on language or dramatic technique

Compare & Contrast

10. How does Priestley present the difference between the older and younger generation through Mr Birling and Eric? Consider:
    - Their attitudes toward responsibility
    - Their responses to the Inspector
    - Priestley's intended message

Character Symbolism

11. What does Eva Smith represent in the play? Why is it significant that she remains offstage? Include:
    - How different characters treat her
    - The social and symbolic purpose she serves
    - How the audience is meant to respond to her silence

For additional practice:

AO1: Choose one character and note how their motivation reflects Edwardian society.

AO2: Pick a quote from their "Key Moments" and analyse how Priestley's language reveals their flaw.

Chapter 4
Contextual Background

A note on Context and the Exam

It is important to note that context is not directly assessed in Section A of Edexcel IGCSE English Literature Paper 2. The assessment criteria for this section focus solely on:

- **AO1**: Demonstrating detailed knowledge and understanding of the text, while presenting a critical and personally engaged response.
- **AO2**: Analysing the writer's use of language, form, and structure to create meaning and achieve effects.

However, a clear understanding of historical, social, and authorial context can support stronger interpretations, particularly when analysing character motivations, thematic development, or dramatic structure. Context should always be used in support of AO1 or AO2, rather than as standalone factual information.

Author Background and Purpose

John Boynton Priestley (1894-1984) was a British writer and social commentator whose experiences during and after the First World War shaped his views on society. As a committed democratic socialist, Priestley believed that society should be more equitable, with responsibility shared across social classes.

Priestley's Purpose in Writing the Play

An Inspector Calls was written in 1945, at the close of the Second World War, and first performed in 1946. However, the play is set in 1912, just before the First World War. This deliberate historical distance allowed Priestley to reflect critically on earlier societal attitudes, especially those concerning class, responsibility, and power. His aim was to encourage audiences to learn from past mistakes and work towards a more just, compassionate society.

The Role of the Inspector

Inspector Goole acts as Priestley's moral voice. Through the Inspector's interrogations, Priestley critiques capitalist values, questions the moral failings of the upper classes, and presents a call for greater social responsibility. The Inspector's speeches often reflect Priestley's personal political beliefs and his desire for post-war social reform.

✏ Extension Task: Write a short speech (75-100 words) that Priestley might deliver today about the need for collective responsibility in society.

✏ Discuss: How do Priestley's personal experiences help explain the message of the play? Discuss with a partner.

Historical, Social, and Political Context

Understanding the significance of the play's dual timeframes —set in 1912 but written and performed after 1945—offers insight into its themes and structural choices.

Britain in 1912

- Society was defined by rigid class divisions, with limited opportunities for social mobility.
- The working class had little protection or representation, and striking for better pay, as Eva Smith did, was often met with dismissal.
- Women were disenfranchised and economically dependent on male relatives or employers.
- The Titanic was regarded as a triumph of engineering and a symbol of British confidence.
- Politicians and businessmen expressed optimism about peace and progress, unaware that the First World War was imminent.

✎ Quick Recap: List three things about life in 1912 Britain that Priestley wanted his audience to question.

Britain in 1945

- The Second World War had ended, leaving the country economically weakened but ideologically changed.
- Wartime experience had fostered a sense of national unity and highlighted the value of shared responsibility.
- There was significant public support for social welfare reforms. The newly elected Labour government

introduced the welfare state, including the National Health Service (NHS) in 1948.
- Priestley, writing in this climate, encouraged audiences to consider how a more cooperative and equitable society might be built.

✏️ Reflection Prompt: Why do you think Priestley set the play in 1912 instead of 1945? What effect does this have on the audience?

Thematic Relevance of Context

Although context is not assessed independently, it underpins many of the play's central themes. When integrated into analysis, it helps explain how Priestley's ideas are communicated and reinforced.

Social Responsibility

Priestley contrasts the individualism of 1912 with the more community-focused values emerging in 1945. The Birlings' refusal to accept responsibility is set against the Inspector's appeal to moral accountability.

Class and Inequality

The experiences of Eva Smith highlight the vulnerability of the working class within a rigid social hierarchy. The contrast between the Birlings and Eva serves as a critique of the economic and social exploitation prevalent in 1912.

Gender Roles

Women had few rights in 1912. Priestley illustrates the consequences of this through Eva's treatment and highlights the shift toward female agency through Sheila's development.

Dramatic Irony and Time

Mr Birling's confident claims about the impossibility of war and the Titanic's safety are knowingly inaccurate to a post-war audience. Priestley uses dramatic irony to challenge complacency and expose flawed thinking.

Moral Judgment and Consequences

The Inspector's speeches and the final twist underscore the play's focus on ethical accountability. The implication that history may repeat itself if lessons are not learned reinforces the idea of moral and social responsibility.

✏️ Extension Task: Choose one theme (e.g. Class, Gender, Responsibility). Write a short paragraph explaining how it links to the time periods of 1912 and 1945.

Structural and Symbolic Elements Supporting Context

1. The play's **cyclical structure**—ending with a second phone call—suggests that failure to change will result in repeated consequences.
2. The **single setting**, confined to the Birlings' dining room, creates a sense of claustrophobia and intense scrutiny, mirroring an interrogation.

3. **Eva Smith's name** is deliberately generic, symbolising the many individuals who suffer under social injustice.
4. The Inspector's **uncertain identity** invites interpretation: he may represent a real inspector, a supernatural presence, or a collective conscience.

Self-Test: Contextual Background

Do keep in mind that context is not strictly examined in this part of the exams. We have included it here to enhance and deepen your understanding of the play and Preistley's intentions in writing it. You can test your understanding of the historical, social, and authorial context surrounding An Inspector Calls.

Multiple Choice Questions

1. Why did Priestley choose to set the play in 1912 rather than in 1945?
    a. He wanted to predict the future
    b. To highlight how little society had changed
    c. To show off his historical knowledge
    d. Because 1912 was a peaceful time
2. What significant event had recently ended when Priestley wrote the play?
    a. World War I
    b. The Industrial Revolution
    c. World War II
    d. The Great Depression

An Inspector Calls

3. The class system in 1912 Britain was characterised by:
   a. Equal opportunities
   b. High taxes for the rich
   c. Limited mobility and rigid structure
   d. Women's voting rights
4. What was the main political message Priestley aimed to communicate through the Inspector?
   a. Support for business growth
   b. Criticism of socialism
   c. Advocacy for social responsibility
   d. Encouragement to join the military

Short Answer Questions

5. What effect might the 1945 audience have felt knowing the First World War happened soon after 1912?
6. How do Priestley's political views influence the character of the Inspector?
7. In what ways does dramatic irony relate to the play's historical setting?
8. How does Eva Smith's story reflect the realities of working-class life in early 20th-century Britain?

Context-Based Tasks

9. Create a timeline of events mentioned in the play or relevant to its context (1912–1945). Include at least 3 historical or political references.
10. Write a short paragraph explaining how an audience in 1945 Britain might respond to the Birlings.
11. List three examples from the play where context supports AO2 analysis of language, form, or structure (e.g. Mr Birling's speeches, the role of the Inspector, the play's ending).

Chapter 5
Main Themes and Key Quotes

An Inspector Calls explores some of the most pressing ideas of Priestley's time, many of which remain urgent today. The play challenges its audience to examine personal conscience, social duty, and the structures of power that shape people's lives. Through carefully constructed scenes and symbolic characters, Priestley delivers a powerful call for responsibility, reform, and reflection.

This section explains the key themes, how they are developed through the plot, and how they connect to Priestley's message. The themes are not isolated — they often overlap, reinforcing the play's wider social vision.

At the end of each theme is a collection of related quotes. Understanding and selecting appropriate quotations is essential for effective literary analysis. In Section A of the Edexcel IGCSE English Literature Paper 2, you are expected to engage closely with the text and support their points using specific evidence. This section presents a selection of key quotations from *An Inspector Calls*, grouped by theme, with brief annotations and guidance on how to remember and use them effectively in exam responses.

While you are allowed to take a clean copy of the play into the exam, familiarity with key lines improves speed, confidence, and the ability to write fluent, structured responses.

Social Responsibility

Overview

At the heart of the play is the question of how much responsibility each person bears for others. Priestley challenges the idea that individuals can live without concern for others. He presents social responsibility as a moral obligation, particularly for those in positions of privilege.

How It Is Developed

- Inspector Goole repeatedly emphasises the interconnectedness of society: *"We are members of one body."*
- Each character is tested on their willingness to accept responsibility for Eva Smith's suffering.
- The younger generation begin to change; the older resist, revealing a generational divide in moral awareness.

Evolution Through the Plot

As the truth about each character's behaviour is revealed, the theme of responsibility intensifies. By the end, only Eric and Sheila have truly internalised the Inspector's message.

Priestley uses this contrast to emphasise the urgent need for societal change.

Key Quotes

"We are members of one body. We are responsible for each other." — Inspector Goole
This line captures Priestley's central message. The use of inclusive pronouns emphasises unity and communal duty, urging the audience to think of society as interconnected.

"Each of you helped to kill her." — Inspector Goole
A blunt and powerful accusation that reinforces shared guilt. The repetition of "each" holds every character accountable and invites the audience to reflect on complicity.

"I can't accept any responsibility." — Mr Birling
Reflects the rigid individualism of the older generation. His refusal to see a connection between his actions and their consequences contrasts with the Inspector's collective view.

"It's simply my fault that in the end she – she committed suicide." — Sheila
Sheila takes full responsibility for her role. The stammered repetition shows emotional distress and an emerging sense of guilt and maturity.

"We all helped to kill her." — Eric
One of the clearest acknowledgements of collective responsibility. Eric's emotional response highlights the moral growth of the younger generation.

"Public men, Mr Birling, have responsibilities as well as privileges." — Inspector Goole

This rebuke underscores the idea that power and influence come with moral obligations. Priestley uses the Inspector to challenge the elite's complacency.

"There are millions and millions and millions of Eva Smiths and John Smiths still left with us." — Inspector Goole

The repetition intensifies the message: Eva's story is not unique. Priestley reminds the audience of ongoing systemic injustice and the need for compassion.

Tip to Remember: Use these quotes when writing about guilt, blame, or moral lessons.

✎ Quick Recap: In your own words, why is Social Responsibility considered the play's central message?

✎ Reflection Prompt: What do the Inspector's lines reveal about Priestley's political beliefs?

✎ Extension Task: Imagine you are delivering a short public service announcement in 1912 on the idea of social responsibility. Write the speech Priestley might have wanted to broadcast.

✎ Extension Task: Write a short monologue from Sheila's perspective after the Inspector leaves. Use two key quotes.

Class and Social Hierarchy

Overview

Priestley critiques the British class system and exposes how it protects the powerful at the expense of the vulnerable.

How It Is Developed

- Each of Eva's interactions with the Birlings reveals a failure of compassion and a sense of superiority.
- Mr Birling views his workers as expendable. Sheila uses her influence to have Eva dismissed. Mrs Birling denies Eva support due to her social status.
- The Inspector's investigation exposes the arrogance and lack of accountability among the upper classes.

Evolution Through the Plot

As the story unfolds, Eva Smith becomes a symbol of how class systems fail individuals. Her anonymity, silence, and suffering stand in sharp contrast to the Birlings' wealth and denial. The Inspector's final speech warns that unless this imbalance is addressed, greater consequences will follow.

Key Quotes

"Girls of that class—" — Mrs Birling
A revealing moment of social prejudice. The abrupt, unfinished sentence implies contempt and moral superiority. Priestley uses it to expose the unspoken assumptions of the upper class.

"She had a lot to say – far too much – so she had to go." — Mr Birling
Birling's dismissal of Eva for speaking up illustrates how the working class is punished for asserting themselves. It shows how those in power silence dissent and maintain control.

"If you don't come down sharply on these people, they'd soon be asking for the earth." — Mr Birling
A stark example of class fear and elitist thinking. Birling sees working-class ambition as dangerous, not legitimate, revealing the threat he perceives in social equality.

"Just used her... as if she was an animal, a thing, not a person." — Inspector Goole
The Inspector condemns the family's treatment of Eva, drawing attention to the dehumanisation of the poor. The comparison strips away any illusion of politeness or decency.

"We are members of one body." — Inspector Goole
Priestley's moral argument against social division. The metaphor of unity undercuts class hierarchy and asserts a shared human responsibility that transcends status.

"She was pretty and a good sport." — Gerald
Gerald's description is patronising and objectifying. It shows how those with privilege reduce working-class women to entertainment or romantic idealisation without true respect.

"She'd lived very economically on what I allowed her." — Gerald
A telling line about control and class. Even in 'helping' Eva, Gerald sees himself as the provider and authority — a

dynamic that reinforces power imbalance rather than removing it.

Tip to Remember: Associate Mr and Mrs Birling with class defensiveness; Gerald with conditional empathy.

✏️ Quick Recap: List three moments where class inequality is shown through action or dialogue.

✏️ Quick Recap: Identify two quotes that expose the Birlings' attitudes toward social class.

✏️ Reflection Prompt: What does Gerald's description of Eva/Daisy suggest about class and power?

✏️ Reflection Prompt: How does Priestley use Eva Smith's story to expose the realities of class division?

Generational Conflict

Overview

Priestley presents a clear contrast between the older and younger characters. The younger generation is portrayed as open-minded and capable of change, while the older generation is shown as resistant and complacent.

How It Is Developed

- Mr and Mrs Birling consistently dismiss the Inspector's message and refuse to alter their views.
- Sheila and Eric, in contrast, express guilt and a desire to take responsibility.
- This divide is central to Priestley's hope that future generations can lead societal reform.

Evolution Through the Plot

The generational gap widens as the play unfolds. Sheila and Eric's reactions are heartfelt, while their parents view the evening as a minor disruption. Priestley uses this divide to place his faith in the youth — and to challenge older attitudes rooted in class and control.

Key Quotes

"Well, I'm old enough to be married, aren't I, and I'm not a child, don't forget." — Sheila
A clear assertion of independence. Sheila challenges the way her parents continue to infantilise her and claims a more adult moral voice.

"You seem to have made a great impression on this child." — Mrs Birling
Patronising tone; seeks to dismiss Sheila's growing independence by framing her as immature. Highlights how the older generation refuses to acknowledge change.

"Why - you fool - he knows. Of course he knows." — Sheila
Signifies Sheila's growing perceptiveness. She understands the Inspector's strategy, showing greater emotional intelligence than her elders.

"You're beginning to pretend now that nothing's really happened at all." — Sheila
Sheila calls out her parents' denial. She is the voice of conscience, determined not to let them evade moral responsibility.

"It frightens me the way you talk." — Sheila
Expresses moral and emotional disapproval. Sheila is disturbed by her parents' unchanged views, showing how far she has grown from their ideology.

"You're not the kind of father a chap could go to when he's in trouble." — Eric
Reveals a lack of emotional support and trust. Priestley criticises Mr Birling's parenting and highlights the disconnect between older authority and younger vulnerability.

"The fact remains that I did what I did." — Eric
Eric accepts responsibility without excuses — a key difference from Mr and Mrs Birling. Confirms moral growth.

"Why – you hysterical young fool – get back – or I'll –" — Mr Birling
The violent outburst exposes Mr Birling's frustration and lack of control. The threat symbolises how the older generation asserts dominance when challenged.

"The famous younger generation who know it all. And they can't even take a joke –" — Mr Birling
A mocking dismissal of younger values. Priestley uses irony here to show Mr Birling's inability to reflect, even after serious revelations.

Tip to Remember: The younger generation accepts guilt; the older generation resists it.

✏️ Quick Recap: What do Sheila and Eric learn by the end of the play that their parents do not?

✏ Extension Task: Write a short dramatic dialogue between Sheila and Mr Birling after the Inspector leaves. Focus on their disagreement about what just happened.

✏ Extension Task: Imagine a future scene: how might Eric challenge his father's views five years later? Write a short script.

✏ Discuss: Why do you think Priestley allows the younger characters to change, but not the older ones?

Gender and Power

Overview

The play highlights how women are affected by both gender and class inequalities. Priestley uses Eva's treatment to show the double vulnerability of working-class women, while Sheila's character marks the potential for change.

How It Is Developed

- Eva is exploited, judged, and dismissed by both men and women in positions of power.
- Gerald and Eric objectify her; Mrs Birling condemns her.
- Sheila's transformation reflects an awakening to both injustice and her own complicity.

Evolution Through the Plot

As the play continues, Sheila's increasing agency contrasts with Eva's powerlessness. Priestley suggests that a more equitable society depends on challenging both gender and class assumptions.

Key Quotes

"She was young and pretty and warm-hearted – and intensely grateful." — Gerald
Gerald's language appears admiring, but also reveals a power imbalance. He frames Eva's worth in terms of appearance and gratitude, highlighting how women's roles were shaped by male desire.

"As if a girl of that sort would ever refuse money!" — Mrs Birling
A deeply prejudiced line. Mrs Birling assumes working-class women are dishonest or greedy, revealing how class and gender combine in moral judgement.

"But these girls aren't cheap labour – they're people." — Sheila
A breakthrough moment. Sheila challenges the dehumanisation of female workers, and begins to express a socially conscious, feminist awareness.

"I hate those hard-eyed dough-faced women." — Gerald
Objectifies women based on looks. Gerald reduces them to physical traits, showing how women are judged and dismissed when they don't conform to standards of beauty.

"Used her for the end of a stupid drunken evening, as if she was an animal, a thing, not a person." — Inspector Goole
Harrowing description of how Eric treated Eva. Priestley

condemns the entitlement and exploitation at the heart of male power in a patriarchal society.

"And you think young women ought to be protected against unpleasant and disturbing things?" — Inspector Goole
A challenge to hypocritical chivalry. The Inspector questions selective protection — a system that shields women only when convenient to men in power.

Tip to Remember: Use Sheila to show progressive gender views; Mrs Birling and Gerald to show inequality.

✏ Quick Recap: Compare Sheila and Eva's experiences in the play. What does their treatment reveal about the role of women in 1912?

✏ Quick Recap: What do Mrs Birling's and Gerald's actions reveal about attitudes towards women?

✏ Reflection Prompt: How do class and gender intersect in Eva's experiences?

Power and Authority

Overview

Priestley critiques how social and institutional power is used — and misused. The play explores who holds power, how it's exercised, and whether it aligns with moral values.

How It Is Developed

- The Birlings and Gerald use status and influence to protect themselves and harm others.

- The Inspector has no legal power, yet speaks with moral authority that shapes the narrative.
- Power is shown to be fragile when built on illusion and denial.

Evolution Through the Plot

The play demonstrates that traditional sources of power—wealth, status, family name—do not equate to moral authority. The Inspector, though lacking in conventional power, holds the strongest influence over the audience and the characters who are willing to change.

Key Quotes

"Public men, Mr Birling, have responsibilities as well as privileges." — Inspector Goole
This line challenges the idea that authority is exempt from accountability. The Inspector's tone is calm but firm, and the balanced phrasing underlines Priestley's belief that status must be matched by social conscience.

"A man has to mind his own business and look after himself." — Mr Birling
This quote summarises capitalist individualism. Birling's values centre on personal gain and self-interest, a philosophy that Priestley strongly critiques through the play.

"I was an alderman for years – and Lord Mayor two years ago – and I'm still on the Bench." — Mr Birling
Birling uses his past titles to assert superiority. Priestley uses this line to expose how the upper class relies on position and tradition rather than moral authority.

"But she died in misery and agony – hating life –" — Inspector Goole
Through stark and emotive imagery, the Inspector exerts moral pressure. His language is blunt and shocking, positioning him as a voice of conscience that overrides social rank.

"We often do on the young ones. They're more impressionable." — Inspector Goole
A subtle but powerful line. The Inspector deliberately targets those more open to change, revealing that true influence lies in shaping minds, not enforcing rules.

"Look, Inspector – I'd give thousands – yes, thousands –" — Mr Birling
A desperate attempt to regain control with money. Priestley shows how the rich try to fix moral failings with wealth, missing the point of justice and human responsibility.

Tip to Remember: These quotes are useful for essays on power, influence, and social critique.

✏ Reflection Prompt: Who holds the most power in the play — and is it always used justly? Support your answer with examples.

✏ Discuss: Which character appears most powerful at the start? And by the end?

✏ Extension Task: Rewrite one of Mr Birling's monologues or speeches to include acknowledgement of social responsibility. How does it change the tone?

🖊 Extension Task: Rewrite one of the Inspector's key speeches from Mr Birling's perspective. How would his version sound?

Truth, Illusion, and Deception

Overview

Priestley explores the gap between appearance and reality — and how characters hide behind false narratives to protect their image.

How It Is Developed

- The Birlings present themselves as a respectable family, but their involvement in Eva's life reveals moral failings.
- Gerald's secret affair, Mr Birling's self-interest and Mrs Birling's public charity work all conceal less honourable motives.
- The Inspector's mysterious identity invites questions about whether the truth matters more than its source.

Evolution Through the Plot

As each façade crumbles, Priestley asks the audience to consider what matters more: the source of truth, or the truth itself. The play warns against comforting illusions — and shows that avoiding responsibility only leads to repetition of harm.

Key Quotes

"You're beginning to pretend now that nothing's really happened at all." — Sheila
Sheila calls out her family's attempt to return to comfort and denial. Her insight reinforces Priestley's warning that ignoring uncomfortable truths leads to moral stagnation.

"There's no Inspector Goole on the police. That man definitely wasn't a police inspector at all." — Gerald
Gerald's focus on the Inspector's identity, rather than his message, reveals a desire to undermine accountability. Priestley uses this to critique those who prioritise appearances over ethics.

"Everything's all right now, Sheila. What about this ring?" — Gerald
Gerald tries to reset the evening, ignoring emotional growth and the seriousness of his actions. His response reveals a failure to grasp the real impact of the night's revelations.

"You're ready to go on in the same old way." — Sheila
Sheila rejects her parents' attempt to erase the past. This line affirms her moral evolution and Priestley's belief that truth must lead to action, not be swept aside.

"I suppose we're all nice people now." — Sheila
A sharply ironic statement. Sheila exposes the hypocrisy of pretending nothing serious occurred, challenging the family's false sense of respectability.

"This girl's still dead, isn't she? Nobody's brought her to life, have they?" — Eric

Eric cuts through the family's relief with a brutal truth. His line reminds the audience that the moral consequences remain, regardless of the Inspector's legitimacy.

Tip to Remember: Use these quotes when exploring denial, moral blindness, and self-deception.

✏️ Quick Recap: Which characters live in denial, and which confront the truth? What effect does this have on the audience?

✏️ Quick Recap: What role does denial play in maintaining the Birlings' illusion of respectability?

✏️ Discuss with a friend: Is the Inspector's identity important? Why or why not?

Change and Redemption

Overview

Priestley offers the possibility of moral growth, particularly through the younger characters, who begin to see the consequences of their actions. He leaves open the possibility of redemption for those who are willing to take responsibility.

How It Is Developed

- Sheila's remorse and Eric's confession signal the potential for transformation.
- Mr and Mrs Birling reject this path, focusing instead on their social standing.

- The Inspector warns that those who fail to learn will be taught in *"fire and blood and anguish."*

Evolution Through the Plot

Redemption is presented as a choice. The play ends with uncertainty—whether the lesson will be learned or ignored. Priestley places that decision in the hands of the audience.

🖉 Reflection Prompt: Do you believe that true change is possible for all characters? Justify your view with evidence from the play.

🖉 Extension Task: Write a short letter from the Inspector to the audience, urging them to act differently from the Birlings.

Key Quotes

"I'll never, never do it again to anybody." — Sheila
An immediate and heartfelt vow. The repetition and straightforward language convey genuine remorse and a strong desire to improve.

"We are still the same people who sat down to dinner here." — Sheila
Sheila urges her family not to dismiss the evening's events. This line reinforces Priestley's view that moral change must come from within, not from external pressure.

"The fact remains that I did what I did." — Eric
Eric refuses to excuse his behaviour, even after the Inspector's identity is questioned. His commitment to responsibility marks a key turning point.

"It's simply my fault that in the end she – she committed suicide." — Sheila

A raw and early admission of guilt. The broken syntax and repetition highlight Sheila's emotional maturity and the start of her moral awakening.

"My God – I'm not likely to forget." — Eric

Eric's visceral reaction shows that the events have affected him deeply. Priestley uses this to contrast the younger generation's emotional growth with the older generation's detachment.

"There's every excuse for what your mother and I did." — Mr Birling

Mr Birling's refusal to accept guilt underlines his resistance to change. This quote exemplifies the complacency Priestley criticises most sharply.

Tip to Remember: These lines help highlight character development and thematic resolution.

✏️ Quick Recap: Which quote best shows a character's growth?

✏️ Reflection Prompt: What is Priestley suggesting about the possibility of redemption?

Themes	Mr Birling	Mrs Birling	Sheila	Eric	Gerald	Inspector Goole	Eva Smith
Social Responsibility	✓	✓	✓	✓		✓	✓
Class and Social Hierarchy	✓	✓			✓	✓	✓
Generational Conflict	✓	✓	✓	✓			
Gender and Power		✓	✓	✓	✓		✓
Power and Authority	✓	✓			✓	✓	
Truth, Illusion, and Deception	✓	✓	✓	✓	✓	✓	
Change and Redemption			✓	✓			

Table 1. This character-theme matrix summarises which themes are most closely associated with each key figure in *An Inspector Calls*.

How to Write About Themes in An Inspector Calls

Most exam questions will ask you to explore either a character or a theme. Even if the question focuses on a character, strong answers often include reference to key themes — like class, responsibility, or power.

To succeed, your writing should:

- Show understanding of how the theme is developed across the play (AO1)
- Explain how Priestley uses language, structure, or character choices to express that theme (AO2)
- Offer an interpretation — not just what happens, but why it matters

Simple Writing Frame

Priestley presents the theme of [theme] through [character/action/scene] by [explanation of technique].

This shows [effect on the audience or Priestley's message], especially when [quote/example].

Sample Paragraph – Theme of Social Responsibility

Priestley presents the theme of social responsibility through Inspector Goole's direct challenge to the Birling family. When he states, "We are members of one body. We are responsible for each other," his use of inclusive pronouns creates a sense of shared moral duty. This line expresses Priestley's belief in community and collective care, especially in contrast to Mr Birling's earlier speech about self-interest. The Inspector's calm authority and repeated emphasis on consequences are used to pressure the characters — and the audience — to consider the impact of their actions on others.

Exam Tip

Avoid just listing themes. Instead, zoom in on how Priestley develops one idea through a moment or character. Link each quote or example back to Priestley's purpose. Use confident verbs: presents, challenges, reveals, warns, contrasts, suggests

Try It Yourself

1. Choose a quote about class or status. How does it reflect the power imbalance in the play — and what might Priestley be criticising?
2. Pick a moment that involves Sheila or Eric. What does it show about the theme of change or redemption, and how does Priestley present the younger generation?
3. Find a quote that shows Mr or Mrs Birling denying responsibility. How does Priestley use their dialogue to explore the play's central message?

4. Write a short paragraph linking the quote "Girls of that class—" to the theme of social hierarchy. What does it reveal about prejudice?

5. Choose a quote from the Inspector. What technique does Priestley use, and how does it reinforce the theme of social responsibility?

Self-Test: Main Themes and Key Quotes

Use this self-test block to consolidate your understanding of the main themes in *An Inspector Calls*. This includes a mix of multiple-choice questions, short answer prompts, and theme-based tasks.

Multiple Choice Questions

1. Which theme is MOST directly expressed in the Inspector's line: "We are members of one body"?
    a. Class Conflict
    b. Gender Roles
    c. Social Responsibility
    d. Truth and Illusion
2. Which character MOST clearly rejects personal responsibility for Eva Smith's fate?
    a. Sheila
    b. Mrs Birling
    c. Eric
    d. The Inspector
3. The theme of gender inequality is shown through:
    a. Sheila's moral growth
    b. Gerald's treatment of Eva
    c. Mr Birling's factory

    d. Eric's confession
4. Which theme is reinforced through the Inspector's final warning of 'fire and blood and anguish'?
　　a. Truth vs Deception
　　b. Class and Power
　　c. Moral Consequence
　　d. Dramatic Irony
5. Which quote BEST expresses the theme of Social Responsibility?
　　a. "A man has to mind his own business."
　　b. "Each of you helped to kill her."
　　c. "As if a girl of that sort would ever refuse money!"
　　d. "We are still the same people who sat down to dinner here."
6. Which quote reveals Mr Birling's capitalist ideology?
　　a. "She was a lively good-looking girl."
　　b. "Public men, Mr Birling, have responsibilities."
　　c. "If you don't come down sharply on these people…"
　　d. "Why – you fool – he knows."

Short Answer Questions

7. What does Priestley suggest about generational conflict through the behaviour of Sheila and her parents?
8. How is Eva Smith used to explore the theme of class inequality?
9. In what way does the Inspector's role challenge traditional ideas of power and authority?
10. What contrast exists between appearance and reality in the way Gerald presents himself?

11. Choose one quote from Eric that shows his acceptance of guilt. What does it reveal about his development?
12. How does Priestley use Mrs Birling's quotes to show her lack of empathy?
13. Select a quote that uses inclusive language. How does it support the play's message?

Longer Tasks

14. Write a paragraph explaining how the theme of redemption is developed through Sheila's character arc.
15. Name the themes for which the following quotes apply (themes: Social Responsibility, Gender and Power, Class Hierarchy):

"But these girls aren't cheap labour – they're people."
"As if a girl of that sort would ever refuse money!"
"Public men, Mr Birling, have responsibilities as well"

16. Choose two of the following themes:
    - Social Responsibility
    - Class and Social Hierarchy
    - Gender and Power
    - Generational Conflict

For each one, write a short paragraph (3–5 sentences) explaining:

- How one character reflects this theme
- One quote that supports your idea
- Why Priestley may have presented the theme this way

Refer back to the section on How to Write About Themes to help you

17. For each statement below, write whether you agree, disagree, or partially agree — and explain why using a quote or reference to a moment in the play.

- Sheila learns more than any other character in the play.
- Mr Birling cares more about reputation than people.
- The Inspector changes nothing.
- Eva Smith is the most powerful character in the play, despite never appearing.
- Priestley believes that real change is only possible for the younger generation.

Chapter 6
Glossary of Key Literary and Dramatic Terms

In order to write clearly, critically, and convincingly about *An Inspector Calls*, you need to use the language of literary analysis. Examiners expect you to identify and comment on how Priestley uses **form**, **structure**, and **language** to shape meaning. This glossary provides definitions of the most relevant terms for analysing dramatic texts at GCSE and IGCSE level.

These terms will help you analyse Priestley's techniques more precisely and meet the requirements of AO2: analysing language, form, and structure. Use this glossary to revise key concepts and improve the depth of your responses.

Language Techniques

Emotive language
Language intended to provoke an emotional response.

Euphemism
A mild or indirect expression used in place of something harsh or blunt.

Hyperbole
Exaggeration for emphasis or dramatic effect.

Inclusive pronouns
Words like "we" or "our" that include speaker and audience, often used to create a sense of unity.

Metaphor
A direct comparison between two unrelated things, stating one is the other.

Monologue
A long speech by a single character to express their thoughts or emotions.

Rhetorical question
A question asked to make a point, not to elicit an answer.

Repetition
The repeated use of a word or phrase for emphasis or effect.

Symbolism
The use of an object, character, or setting to represent a larger idea.

Tone
The attitude or emotional quality conveyed by the writer or a character.

Structure and Plot

Cyclical Structure
A narrative or plot that ends where it begins, reinforcing repeated ideas or consequences.

Climactic Structure
A traditional plot with rising (a build-up of) tension, a crisis point, and a resolution.

Foreshadowing
Hints or clues about events that will occur later in the play.

Juxtaposition
The placement of two elements side by side to highlight contrast.

Motif
A recurring image, symbol, or idea that reinforces a central theme.

Real-time narrative
A structure in which events unfold continuously without time jumps.

Sequential revelations
Plot developments revealed step-by-step to build suspense.

Unity of setting
The action remains in one location, enhancing focus and intensity.

Dramatic Form and Devices

Didactic
A text that teaches a moral or political lesson.

Dramatic Irony
When the audience knows more than the characters, creating tension or humour.

Entrances and exits
The timing of characters arriving or leaving the stage to influence events.

Exposition
Background information revealed at the start of a play.

Fourth wall
The imaginary wall between the audience and the actors; breaking it engages the audience directly.

Stage Directions
Instructions in the script about movement, expression, lighting, or setting.

Subtext
The underlying meaning behind a character's words or actions.

Theatrical devices
Techniques used to enhance the audience's experience (e.g., lighting, pauses, props).

Literary Concepts and Critical Terms

Allusion
A brief reference to another text, event, or cultural idea.

Conflict
The tension or struggle between characters or opposing forces.

Moral Responsibility
The duty to act ethically and accept the consequences of one's actions.

Protagonist
The main character in the play whose decisions shape the narrative.

Social Commentary
When a text critiques societal values, injustice, or inequality.

Theme
A central idea or message explored in the play.

Tricolon
A series of three parallel elements used for emphasis or rhythm.

Using This Glossary as You Write

This glossary gives you the language to write clearly and accurately about *An Inspector Calls*. Each term can help you explain what Priestley is doing — how he creates meaning through structure, language, and dramatic technique.

You are **not expected to memorise or use every single term**. Start by choosing a few that make sense to you — ones that help you explain your ideas more precisely. You'll find that some techniques come up often in the play, like *dramatic irony*, *symbolism*, and *repetition*. These are a good place to begin.

Use this glossary whenever you plan or review your work. You'll find it especially helpful in the sections that follow — on structure, analysis, and essay writing. Over time, using these terms will make your writing feel more confident and focused.

What matters most is using the terms that help you explain ideas clearly and thoughtfully, in a way that shows your understanding of the play.

Self-test: Glossary of Literary and Dramatic Terms

Multiple Choice Questions

Choose the most accurate answer for each question:

1. What does *dramatic irony* involve?
    a. An object representing a deeper idea
    b. The audience knowing more than the characters
    c. A play with a sad ending
    d. An actor forgetting their lines
2. Which term describes a structure that ends where it begins?
    a. Climatic structure
    b. Linear plot
    c. Cyclical structure
    d. Repetition
3. What is *foreshadowing*?
    a. A type of conflict between characters
    b. A narrative that repeats itself
    c. Hints or clues about future events
    d. A long speech by one character

An Inspector Calls

Short Answer Questions

Answer each in one or two sentences:

4. What is the difference between *stage directions* and *dialogue*?
5. Give an example of *symbolism* from a dramatic text you've studied.
6. Why is *subtext* important when analysing character interaction?

Fill in the Blanks

7. A _____ is a repeated image or phrase that helps reinforce a theme.
8. The term _____ refers to when a character speaks alone at length, revealing inner thoughts.
9. *Juxtaposition* is used to highlight _____ between two ideas or characters.

Reflection Prompt

10. Which three terms do you find most useful for writing about drama, and how will you apply them in your next essay?

Chapter 7
Language, Form and Structure

Section A of the Edexcel IGCSE English Literature Paper 2 explicitly requires you to analyse how writers use **language, form, and structure** to create meanings and effects. This is the essence of **Assessment Objective 2 (AO2)** and is present in every exam question, regardless of theme or character focus. This section explores how Priestley uses specific techniques in *An Inspector Calls* to shape the play's message, enhance dramatic impact, and influence audience response.

When writing about *An Inspector Calls*, remember it is a play written for performance. You are analysing both Priestley's language and his stagecraft, how lighting, pauses, entrances, and the single setting shape audience response.

How to Use This Section

This section includes lots of useful techniques — more than you will need in any one essay. You are not expected to use every idea. Start with a few techniques that you understand clearly and practise writing about them. In your exam, focus on choosing **just a small number of your favourite techniques** and linking them to the question and theme.

Language

Priestley's language choices are deliberate and often symbolic. He uses a combination of persuasive, emotive, and ironic language to reveal character, develop theme, and critique social attitudes.

The table below provides the name of a language technique compared to its example and the effect it causes. This list is very comprehensive and by no means all necessary at GCSE level. We would recommend picking out a few of your favourite a committing them to memory. With time and practise, you will start to find it easier to recognise and name these when you are reading the text.

Key Techniques and Examples

Colloquial/period speech
"Hard-headed businessman" / "fiddlesticks!"
Effect: Reflects the era and class distinctions; captures arrogance and traditionalism.

Dramatic irony
"The Titanic... unsinkable, absolutely unsinkable." ~ Mr Birling
Effect: Undermines Birling's authority; signals flawed optimism and hubris.

Emotive language
"She died in misery and agony – hating life." — Inspector Goole
Effect: Creates pathos, engaging audience sympathy and moral judgement.

Euphemism
"A girl of that class" — Mrs Birling
Effect: Masks prejudice and judgement in polite language; reveals underlying bigotry.

Hyperbole
"They'd soon be asking for the earth." — Mr Birling
Effect: Exaggerates to mock working-class ambition; exposes capitalist fears and classism.

Imperatives
"Don't stammer and yammer at me again, man!" — Inspector Goole
Effect: Conveys power and moral authority; cuts through denial and evasion.

Inclusive pronouns
"We are members of one body." — Inspector Goole
Effect: Reinforces unity and social duty; makes audience feel collectively responsible.

Juxtaposition
Young vs old, Inspector vs Mr Birling
Effect: Highlights moral and ideological contrasts within the play.

Metaphor
"Chain of events" !" — Inspector Goole
Effect: Suggests interconnectedness and consequences; a motif for cause and effect.

Paradox
"You're beginning to pretend now that nothing's really happened at all." — Sheila
Effect: Exposes the contradiction between appearance and reality in the Birlings' reactions

Rhetorical questions
"Why shouldn't they try for higher wages?" — Eric
Effect: Challenges authority and provokes thought, especially around class and labour.

Repetition
"Never, never do it again to anybody." — Sheila
Effect: Reinforces emotional sincerity and moral transformation.

Symbolic language
"Fire and blood and anguish" !" ~ Inspector Goole
Effect: Apocalyptic (biblical) warning that symbolises social upheaval and consequences of inaction.

Tone and register shifts
Mr Birling's smug tone vs Inspector's solemnity
Effect: Changes in tone reflect shifts in power, tension, and moral weight.

📌 **Exam Tip:** Focus on how Priestley's word choices create tone and character. For top marks, always explain *why* a word or phrase is effective, not just what it means.

Sentence Starters for Writing About Language

These sentence frames can help you write about Priestley's language choices more clearly.

Priestley uses [technique] to show that...

- *This creates a feeling of...*
- *The word/phrase "[quote]" suggests that...*
- *This helps the audience understand...*

This supports the theme of...

Try using one or two of these when writing about a character or theme.

How to Apply a Language Technique in an Essay

Knowing the technique is only part of AO2 — you also need to explain how it works in the play and what effect it has. Here's an example of how to write about language using a clear, exam-style paragraph.

Priestley uses emotive language and inclusive pronouns in the Inspector's final speech to strengthen his moral authority. When he says, *"We are members of one body. We are responsible for each other,"* the word *"we"* draws the audience into his message, making the call for responsibility feel collective. This reinforces Priestley's central theme that society must care for its most vulnerable and positions the Inspector as the voice of conscience.

Extension Challenge

1. Try this yourself: Choose a quote spoken by Sheila or Eric. Identify the technique, then write a short paragraph explaining how it affects the audience and links to a theme

2. How would Priestley's message change if the Inspector spoke in softer, less direct language? Re-write one of his key lines with a different tone.

Form

An Inspector Calls is written as a stage play and follows the conventions of **well-made drama** with a moral purpose. Its form combines elements of social realism, detective fiction, and moral drama that directly supports Priestley's social commentary. It is also a modern *tragicomedy* a serious story with moments of irony and moral reckoning.

Understanding the dramatic form of *An Inspector Calls* helps you analyse how Priestley constructs meaning beyond the dialogue itself. While there are many features at play, you do not need to remember every term to succeed. Focus on a few that you can clearly explain and connect to Priestley's message. With repeated exposure and practice, recognising how form shapes the audience's experience will become familiar in your analysis.

Dramatic Form Features

Aside
A brief remark spoken directly to the audience, but seemingly to himself or herself. It reveals a character's thoughts or true feelings.

Climactic structure
The plot builds to key revelations and the Inspector's final speech, creating dramatic tension and moral impact.

Didactic purpose
The play is designed to teach a moral lesson about responsibility and social justice, reflecting Priestley's socialist ideals.

Entrances and exits as cues
Characters appear at strategic moments (e.g. the Inspector's arrival), structuring the play and amplifying tension.

Fourth wall manipulation
The Inspector appears to speak on Priestley's behalf, sometimes addressing the audience directly through tone and message.

Hamartia
An ancient Greek theatre term that means error, frailty, or mistaken judgment which causes the fortunes of the hero in a tragedy to be reversed; a personal flaw that leads to downfall. For e.g. Mr Birling's pride, Mrs Birling's prejudice.

Pathetic fallacy
When nature, the weather or setting, reflects the mood, theme or political condition of society of the characters — e.g. lighting shifts from "pink and intimate" to "brighter and harder."

Real-time narrative
The play unfolds over a single evening in real time, creating a sense of urgency and limiting escape from scrutiny.

Single setting
All action takes place in the Birlings' dining room, adding claustrophobia and intensifying the moral atmosphere.

Stagecraft, theatrical and performance devices
Use of exits, lighting shifts (e.g., "pink and intimate" to "brighter and harder"), and pauses enhance dramatic effect.

- *Lighting:* The shift from "pink and intimate" to "brighter and harder" mirrors the family's loss of comfort and the Inspector's moral scrutiny.
- *Sound:* The "sharp ring of the doorbell" cuts through Birling's speech about self-reliance, symbolising interruption of complacency.
- *Pauses and silences:* Used throughout interrogations to build tension and discomfort.
- *Entrances and exits:* The Inspector's timing controls the rhythm of revelations; Sheila's return in Act 2 exposes emotional fallout.
- *Props:* The port and whisky represent wealth and denial; their rejection by the Inspector symbolises moral cleansing.

Suspense and delayed revelation
Each character's link to Eva is uncovered one by one, mimicking detective fiction and holding the audience's focus.

Symbolic character roles
Characters represent social archetypes (e.g. capitalist, worker, inspector), reinforcing themes over individual realism.

Unity of time and place
Adheres closely to the classical unities, focusing the audience's attention and increasing dramatic tension.

Offstage action
Key events occur offstage (e.g. Eva's death), prompting the audience to imagine consequences and judge characters.

Open ending
The unresolved final twist invites audience reflection and reinforces the ongoing relevance of Priestley's message.

Sentence Starters for Writing About Form

When writing about the play as drama (form), try these phrases:

Priestley presents the play as a stage drama to...

- *The use of [feature] makes the audience feel...*
- *This helps focus the audience's attention on...*
- *This feature adds dramatic effect by...*

This supports Priestley's aim to...

How to Apply a Form Feature in an Essay

Priestley uses a **single setting** — the Birlings' dining room — to keep all the characters under scrutiny throughout the play. This adds tension and a sense of moral pressure, as no one can escape or avoid what's being revealed. The formal structure of a stage play supports Priestley's aim to hold a mirror up to society and force the audience to reflect on their own values.

📌 Exam Tip:

Link the dramatic form directly to audience impact. For example, how does the use of one setting create a sense of pressure or moral entrapment?

✏️ Discuss:

Discuss with a partner: Why do you think Priestley chose to keep the Inspector on stage for almost the entire play? What effect does this have?

Structure

The structure of *An Inspector Calls* plays a critical role in conveying Priestley's themes and sustaining dramatic tension. Priestley combines large-scale structural choices (macro-structure) with small-scale devices (micro-structure) to shape audience understanding, reveal character flaws, and promote social change.

He also sustains tension through constant conflict, between generations, social classes, and moral beliefs. The Inspector's calm authority contrasts with the Birlings' defensive hostility, creating dramatic conflict that drives the play. Each revelation heightens uncertainty and emotional pressure. This tension keeps the audience engaged while forcing them to judge the characters' actions and reflect on their own social conscience.

Understanding these techniques will help strengthen your AO2 analysis and also help you write with more precision. This list includes the most important structural elements to know. However, you do not need to memorise everything — start by becoming familiar with a few that are obvious to you and practise using them in your essay writing.

Dramatic Structure Overview

Like many stage plays, *An Inspector Calls* follows a clear dramatic pattern that guides the audience through tension, revelation, and resolution. Knowing this structure will help you describe how Priestley organises ideas and builds momentum throughout the play:

Stage	Description	Example
I Exposition	Introduces setting, mood, and key characters.	The opening dinner scene establishes the Birlings' confidence, wealth, and ignorance.
II Rising Action	Conflict and tension increase through new information and interrogation.	The Inspector's questioning of each character exposes hidden guilt.
III Climax	The highest point of tension or revelation.	Eric's confession and the Inspector's moral speech.
IV Falling Action	Characters react to the crisis; tension shifts toward reflection.	The Inspector leaves; guilt and denial divide the family.
V Denouement (Resolution)	The play's conclusion, often including a twist or moral reckoning.	The phone call announcing a real inspector re-ignites the tension and completes the cycle.

Table 2. This 5-part structure reflects Priestley's control over pace and revelation. Each act tightens the pressure before offering brief relief, only for the final twist to reset the audience's perspective.

Cliffhanger
Example: Final phone call interrupts the family's relief
Purpose/Effect: Keeps the audience engaged after the curtain falls; demands moral reflection

Contrast and juxtaposition
Example: Youth vs age; denial vs guilt; illusion vs truth
Purpose/Effect: Highlights ideological differences between characters and reinforces key themes

Cyclical ending
Example: The play ends with a second phone call about a real inspector
Purpose/Effect: Creates a sense of inevitable consequence; suggests history will repeat if lessons aren't learned

Dramatic foil
Example: Mr Birling vs. The Inspector
Purpose/Effect: A character who contrasts with another to highlight differences

Epiphany
Example: Sheila and Eric's acceptance of guilt
Purpose/Effect: A sudden realisation that leads to change

Nemesis (Poetic justice)
Example: The Birlings' relief overturned by the final phone call
Purpose/Effect: When characters face consequences fitting their moral failings

Real-time action
Example: The entire play occurs over one evening without time jumps
Purpose/Effect: Increases pressure on characters; heightens dramatic immediacy

Repetition and echoing
Example: Key phrases (e.g., "responsibility", "we are members of one body") recur throughout
Purpose/Effect: Reinforces the play's moral message; shows who accepts or rejects the Inspector's teaching

Sequential revelations
Example: The Inspector reveals each character's connection to Eva one by one
Purpose/Effect: Builds dramatic tension; allows moral judgement to build gradually

Unity of setting
Example: All scenes take place in the Birlings' dining room
Purpose/Effect: Creates claustrophobia; allows for uninterrupted scrutiny and tension

Use of tension arcs
Example: Mr Birling's confrontation with the Inspector (Act 1) and Eric's outburst against his mother (Act 3)
Purpose/Effect: Each act ends with a moment of high tension (e.g., new revelation, Inspector's speech). Keeps pace taut; propels narrative forward and holds audience attention

Sentence Starters for Writing About Structure

When writing about how the structure shapes meaning, you can use the following as a guide:

Priestley structures the play so that...

- *This moment is placed here to...*
- *This builds tension by...*
- *The repetition of [word/idea] reinforces...*

The structure encourages the audience to...

📌 Exam Tip

When writing about structure, consider how the play builds or releases tension and how repetition or contrast affects the audience.

How to Apply a Structural Technique in an Essay

Priestley uses a **cyclical ending** to show that the Birlings have not learned their lesson. Just after they begin to dismiss the Inspector's visit, the phone rings again — this time, a real inspector is on the way. This structure suggests that if people refuse to take responsibility, history will repeat itself. It reinforces Priestley's message that change is needed in society.

✏️ Quick Recap Task:

List three structural features Priestley uses and explain how each one supports the play's message.

🖊 **Reflection Prompt:**

Which moment in the play had the biggest structural impact on you as a reader?

AO2 Starter Pack – Good Techniques to Learn First

These are useful in many questions and easy to apply:

- **Language:** Dramatic irony, emotive language, symbolism
- **Form:** Single setting, didactic purpose, offstage action
- **Structure:** Sequential revelations, cyclical ending, contrast

Try to use **one from each group** in your writing.

Other Key Phrases for AO2 Analysis

You can also use the following sentence stems to support effective AO2 commentary:

- *Priestley uses this word/line to suggest...*
- *This moment increases tension because...*
- *The structure of the scene reinforces...*
- *The audience is positioned to...*
- *The contrast between X and Y reveals...*

Self-test: Language, Form and Structure

Multiple Choice Questions:

1. What is the effect of dramatic irony in Mr Birling's speeches?
   a. It makes him more trustworthy
   b. It highlights his ignorance
   c. It reduces tension
   d. It supports the Inspector
2. What is the significance of the single setting of the dining room?
   a. It shows the family's wealth
   b. It keeps costume changes simple
   c. It increases moral and emotional pressure
   d. It allows Eva Smith to appear

Short Answer Tasks:

3. Identify one example of emotive language and explain its effect.
4. What is meant by a cyclical structure, and how does Priestley use it?

Explain & Explore:

5. How does the contrast between the older and younger generations in the play reinforce Priestley's message?
6. Choose one structural or dramatic feature and explain

Chapter 8
How to write your essays

Using a Structure to Plan and Write Effective Essays

In Section A of Edexcel IGCSE English Literature Paper 2, students are required to write a 30-mark essay that demonstrates close understanding of the text (AO1) and analysis of the writer's methods (AO2). This sub-section provides a structured approach to answering exam-style questions, helping students progress from initial planning to analytical writing through a three-step process.

Step 1: Understand the Question

Begin by identifying the key focus of the question. This may relate to:

- A specific character (e.g. Sheila, Mr Birling)
- A theme (e.g. responsibility, power, class)
- A dramatic feature (e.g. structure, irony, symbolism)

Ask yourself:

- What is the question really asking me to explore?
- What does Priestley want the audience to understand or feel?

Step 2: Select Quotations

Choose three to five quotations from across the play that:

- Clearly relate to the focus of the question
- Offer opportunities to explore language, structure, or dramatic technique
- Reflect character development or thematic significance

Quotations should be concise and specific — long passages are rarely needed.

Step 3: Plan and Write Using PEEL or PETAL

Writing analytical paragraphs is a key part of responding to essay questions in Edexcel IGCSE English Literature. You should aim to write **three to four well-developed paragraphs** in your 30-mark essay.

There are two structures you can use, depending on your confidence and level of analysis:

Step 3A: PEEL (For Developing Writers)

The PEEL structure is ideal if you are building confidence with essay writing. It focuses on making a clear point, supporting it with evidence, and explaining its meaning in relation to the question.

Point - Make a clear statement that answers the question.

Evidence - Support your point with a relevant quote.

Explanation - Explain what the quote shows about the character or theme.

Link - Connect back to the question or Priestley's purpose.

Worked Example Using PEEL

Question

'Mrs Birling shows no real understanding of what she has done.'

How does Priestley present her character?

Sample Paragraph (Step 3A – PEEL):

Mrs Birling is shown as someone who refuses to accept responsibility. She says, *"I accept no blame for it at all,"* which shows that she does not feel guilty for her actions. This suggests that she believes she is above being questioned, and does not think her choices have consequences. Priestley presents her this way to show how the upper class can be cold and uncaring, especially towards people like Eva Smith.

PEEL Sentence Starters

P: Priestley shows that…

E: This is shown when…

E: This suggests that…

L: This shows Priestley's message that…

Final Tip for Practice

Use **PEEL** when you're getting started with essay writing, especially if you're working on:

- Structuring clear points
- Building confidence in using quotations
- Practising linking ideas back to the theme or question

As you improve, aim to include **technique identification** and **deeper analysis**, which you can do by transitioning to PETAL.

Step 3B: PETAL (For Higher-Level Analysis)

The **PETAL** Paragraph Structure

Point - Make a clear statement in response to the question.

Evidence - Provide a relevant quote from the text.

Technique - Identify a literary or dramatic technique used in the quotation.

Analysis - Explain how the technique creates meaning or affects the audience.

Link - Connect back to the question or explain Priestley's broader purpose.

Worked Example Using PETAL

Question:

'Mrs Birling shows no real understanding of what she has done.'

How does Priestley present her character?

Planning Notes (Step 1):

- Represents the privileged upper class
- Shows moral detachment and prejudice
- Resists learning from the Inspector

Quotation Bank (Step 2):

- *"I accept no blame for it at all."*
- *"Girls of that class—"*
- *"Go and look for the father of the child. It's his responsibility."*

Sample Paragraph (Step 3B – PETAL):

Priestley presents Mrs Birling as a character who refuses to accept moral responsibility. This is evident when she states, *"I accept no blame for it at all."* The use of emphatic language and formal tone emphasises her detachment and moral arrogance. The line reflects her belief in her own superiority and her failure to engage with the consequences of her actions. Priestley uses this portrayal to criticise the complacency of the upper classes and reinforce the theme of social irresponsibility. Her refusal to change aligns her with those who allow injustice to continue unchecked.

PETAL Sentence Starters

You may find these sentence frames helpful when planning:

- **Point**: Priestley presents [character/theme] as...
- **Evidence**: This is shown when [quote]...
- **Technique**: The use of [technique] suggests...

- **Analysis**: This implies... / This highlights... / This makes the audience consider...
- **Link**: This supports Priestley's message about... / It reinforces the theme of...

Final Tip for Practice

Aim to write three to four PETAL paragraphs in a 30-mark essay. Each should offer a distinct point and build towards a coherent argument. Practice by drafting one paragraph per session, then combining them into full essays.

Sample Essay Plans

Before writing a full essay, it's important to create a plan that structures your response clearly and logically. A strong essay plan:

- Helps you stay focused on the question
- Ensures each paragraph builds your argument
- Allows you to balance your analysis across different parts of the play

This section provides a model plan for a commonly asked theme-based question. Each plan outlines three key paragraphs, showing how to build a thoughtful and exam-ready response.

Example Plan: Theme-Based Question

Question:

How does Priestley explore the theme of responsibility in An Inspector Calls?

Introduction

Briefly define "responsibility" in the context of the play.

Mention that Priestley presents it as a moral issue, using characters to model both acceptance and rejection of social responsibility.

Paragraph 1 – Mr Birling's Denial of Responsibility

- Quote: *"I can't accept any responsibility."*
- Technique: Emphatic denial; irony
- Analysis: Shows his selfishness and disconnect from social change
- Link: Represents capitalist values Priestley criticises

Paragraph 2 – Sheila's Acceptance and Growth

- Quote: *"I'll never, never do it again to anybody."*
- Technique: Repetition; emotional tone
- Analysis: Shows how younger generation is more open to learning
- Link: Priestley presents Sheila as a model for change

Paragraph 3 – Inspector as the Moral Voice

- Quote: *"We are members of one body."*
- Technique: Collective pronouns; didactic tone
- Analysis: Reinforces Priestley's message of social unity
- Link: Intended to influence post-war audience attitudes

Conclusion

Summarise up how responsibility is central to the play.

Highlight the contrast between characters who change and those who don't, reinforcing Priestley's call for a more compassionate society.

Skeleton Structures for Essay Responses

A skeleton essay structure provides a clear blueprint for writing analytical responses. It ensures your essay stays focused, covers Assessment Objectives (AO1 and AO2), and flows logically from introduction to conclusion. Use these templates as a starting point for any theme or character question.

Essay Skeleton: General Format

1. Introduction

Set the focus of your essay and define the theme or character. Mention Priestley's purpose and the play's overall message.

Template:

In *An Inspector Calls*, Priestley explores the theme of [insert theme] through [insert character(s)/event(s)]. The play is used as a critique of [insert social issue]. This essay will examine how Priestley uses [language/form/structure] to present [theme].

2. Body Paragraphs (3-4 PETAL paragraphs)

Each paragraph should:

- Introduce one clear idea
- Use a quotation as evidence
- Identify a literary or dramatic technique
- Analyse the effect
- Link back to Priestley's message

Paragraph Starter Template (PETAL):

- **Point**: Priestley presents [character/theme] as...
- **Evidence**: This is shown when [quote]...
- **Technique**: The use of [technique] suggests...
- **Analysis**: This implies... / It highlights... / This creates the impression that...
- **Link**: This reinforces Priestley's message that...

Repeat this structure for each new point, ideally covering:

- One character who resists change
- One who develops
- A structural or symbolic device (e.g. Inspector, setting, timing)

3. Conclusion

Return to the question and sum up Priestley's message.

Example:

In conclusion, Priestley uses [character/device/theme] to present a strong critique of [insert issue]. Through the characters' actions and the Inspector's message, the audience is encouraged to [insert interpretation]. The play leaves us questioning our own role in society and how we treat others.

Why Use This Structure

This structure gives you the flexibility to adapt their ideas while ensuring their essay meets the criteria for clear, critical, and focused analysis.

Chapter 10 Practice Questions contains a range of sample questions organised by theme. Use these to practise writing essay plans and eventually full essays.

Planning Templates

Effective essays begin with thoughtful planning. This section provides **printable and reusable templates** to help you organise your ideas before you start writing. Planning allows you to:

- Stay focused on the question
- Select relevant evidence and techniques
- Build logical, structured responses
- Ensure each paragraph contributes to your overall argument

These templates can be used for timed practice, homework, or pre-writing exercises in class.

How to Use It

- Start with the **essay question** and work downward.
- Fill in the quote bank early as this helps guide the points you'll make.
- Match each point to a character or event that supports it.
- Decide which **literary or dramatic techniques** you'll highlight.
- Use your plan to guide a PETAL or PEEL-based essay.

Essay Planning Template: Use this structure to map out your response before you write.

Essay Question:

Theme/Focus of Question:

Key Message/Priestley's Purpose:

Quote Bank (3–5 key quotes)

1.

2.

3.

4.

5.

An Inspector Calls

Paragraph 1 – Main Point

Linked Character/Theme/Event

Technique(s) to Include

Paragraph 2 – Main Point

Linked Character/Theme/Event

Technique(s) to Include

Paragraph 3 – Main Point

Linked Character/Theme/Event

Technique(s) to Include

Conclusion – Final Message

How will you summarise Priestley's message and the character/theme's role?

Chapter 9
Quick Recap Tools

This section provides concise revision tasks to help you consolidate your understanding of *An Inspector Calls*. The following exercises support retention of key content and are designed to be used independently or as part of classroom review.

Each activity reinforces core areas of the play including key quotes, characters, themes, and structural features while also preparing you for common exam requirements.

Revision Checklist

You should be confident in each of the following areas before the exam. Use this checklist to identify strengths and revision priorities.

An Inspector Calls

Area of Knowledge

- Understand the central message of the play
- Identify and explain the play's key themes
- Know the role and development of each major character
- Recall 3–5 quotations for each theme and character
- Recognise Priestley's use of dramatic irony and structure
- Explain how the Inspector functions as a moral force
- Analyse how language, form and structure create meaning
- Apply PETAL structure to write developed paragraphs
- Identify key events in the plot and their dramatic function

Fill-in-the-Blanks – Key Quotes

Complete the quotations using your knowledge of the play:

1. *"We are members of one _____."*
2. *"The _____ is not the important thing. It's what happened to the girl and what we all did to her that matters."*
3. *"There are millions and millions of Eva Smiths and _____ Smiths still left with us."*
4. *"But these girls aren't cheap _____ – they're people."*
5. *"She was a lively good-looking girl – country-bred, I fancy – and she'd had a lot to say – far too much – so she had to go."* (Who said this? _____)
6. *"I suppose we're all nice people now."* (Spoken by: _____)

Final Multiple Choice Questions

1. What theme is MOST closely linked with the character of Sheila?
   a. Justice
   b. Responsibility and change
   c. Gender inequality
   d. Deception
2. Mr Birling's confidence in the future is undermined by:
   a. The stage directions
   b. Dramatic irony
   c. Foreshadowing
   d. Symbolism
3. Which of the following is NOT a theme explored in the play?
   a. Forgiveness
   b. Social class
   c. Responsibility
   d. Generational conflict
4. What effect does the Inspector's final speech have on the audience?
   a. Creates suspense
   b. Offers comic relief
   c. Delivers Priestley's moral message
   d. Introduces a new plot twist
5. The structure of the play is best described as:
   a. Episodic
   b. Cyclical
   c. Non-linear
   d. Flashback-driven

Final Writing Practice

Use the PETAL structure to write a paragraph answering:

Question:

How does Priestley use the character of Eric to explore generational conflict?

Your paragraph should include:

- A clear point
- A relevant quote
- A named technique
- Analysis of meaning and effect
- A link to Priestley's message or the question

If you're not ready yet, don't worry

- Review your **quote banks**
- Revisit **character profiles and themes** in Chapters 3 and 5
- Return to the **essay planning templates** in Chapter 8

Use this guide to help you revise actively, test yourself regularly, and go into your exam prepared and confident.

Chapter 10
Practice Exam Questions

The best way to build confidence in your exam responses is through regular, focused practice. This section gives you a chance to apply everything you've learned — from understanding characters and themes to using language, form, and structure in your writing.

You don't need to write full essays every time. Start by planning your response, choosing relevant quotes, or writing just one strong paragraph. With each step, you'll become more familiar with how exam questions are phrased and how to approach them clearly and calmly.

Use the observed trends below to guide your revision. You'll notice that some types of questions come up again and again — and that's a good thing. The more you practise, the more prepared you will be.

Observed Trends

Recurring Themes: Social responsibility and class dynamics are frequently examined, reflecting the play's central concerns.

Character Focus: Questions often centre on key figures such as Sheila, Mr. Birling, and the Inspector, allowing for in-depth character analysis.

Thematic Pairings: Exams typically offer a choice between a theme-based question and a character-based question, enabling you to select based on your strengths.

Revision Tips

Thematic Preparation: Organise revision materials by theme to facilitate targeted study sessions.

Quote Integration: Associate key quotations with specific themes to enhance analytical responses.

Practice Essays: Write practice essays for each theme to develop a versatile approach to potential exam questions.

Social Responsibility

Explore the theme of responsibility for others in An Inspector Calls.
You must consider language, form and structure in your answer.

Gerald: "I don't come into this suicide business."
To what extent does Gerald Croft accept responsibility in the play?
You must consider language, form and structure in your answer.

How does Priestley present characters who refuse to change in the play?
You must consider language, form and structure in your answer.
(Also relevant to Generational Conflict & Redemption)

Class and Social Hierarchy

Explore how Priestley uses the setting of the play to develop his themes.
You must consider language, form and structure in your answer.
(Linked to Structure and Power)

Explore the role of Edna in the play and what she might symbolise.
You must consider language, form and structure in your answer.
(Also relevant to Gender and Power)

How does Priestley encourage the audience to feel sympathy for Eva Smith?
You must consider language, form and structure in your answer.

Eva Smith never appears on stage, yet she is central to the play.
How does Priestley make her presence felt?
You must consider language, form and structure in your answer.

Generational Conflict

Eric Birling is a more honest character than he first appears.
How far do you agree with this view of Eric?
You must consider language, form and structure in your answer.

How does Priestley present characters who refuse to change in the play?
You must consider language, form and structure in your answer.
(Also relevant to Social Responsibility)

Gender and Power

'*Mrs Birling shows no real understanding of what she has done.*'
How does Priestley present her character?
You must consider language, form and structure in your answer.

Explore the Edna's role in the play and what she might symbolise.
You must consider language, form and structure in your answer.
(Also relevant to Class)

Power and Authority

In what ways is Mr Birling shown to be a man who values reputation above truth?
You must consider language, form and structure in your answer.

How does Priestley present the Inspector as a challenge to the Birling family?
You must consider language, form and structure in your answer.

Truth, Illusion and Deception

How does Priestley explore the theme of denial in An Inspector Calls?
You must consider language, form and structure in your answer.

Explore how Priestley uses dramatic irony to influence the audience's perception of the characters.
You must consider language, form and structure in your answer.

Justice and Consequence

How is the idea of justice explored in the play?
You must consider language, form and structure in your answer.

Change and Redemption

To what extent do the younger characters offer hope for the future?
You must consider language, form and structure in your answer.

How is character development used to reinforce Priestley's message?
You must consider language, form and structure in your answer.

Dramatic Form and Structure

How does Priestley use structure and stagecraft to increase tension in the play?
You must consider language, form and structure in your answer.

Explore how the use of a single setting contributes to the message of the play.
You must consider language, form and structure in your answer.

Symbolism and Interpretation

How does Priestley use symbolism to communicate key ideas in the play?
You must consider language, form and structure in your answer.

'The Inspector is more of a symbol than a man.'
How far do you agree with this view?
You must consider language, form and structure in your answer.

Download: *An Inspector Calls* – Past Exam Questions by Theme (Ebook)

As you have purchased this revision guide, you can download our companion booklet — *Past Exam Questions by Theme* — free of charge from our publisher's website.

To access your free copy:

1. Visit: **www.bailbrooklane.com**
2. Navigate to An Inspector Calls Past Year Exam Questions by Theme
3. Click **Add to Basket**
4. On the basket page, enter the coupon code: **AICPASTQUES**
5. Click **Apply Coupon** — the price will reduce to £0
6. Proceed to **Checkout**, enter your details, and place your order
7. You will receive an email with a secure download link.

You may download the ebook **up to two times**. If you have any difficulty accessing your copy, please contact: **info@bailbrooklane.com**

Chapter 11
Further Reading and Resources

While this guide is designed to provide a complete and exam-focused approach to *An Inspector Calls*, deepening your understanding through wider reading can offer valuable perspective and sharpen your critical thinking. Exploring additional resources allows you to:

- See how others interpret characters, structure, and themes
- Understand the historical and political background of the play in greater depth
- Familiarise yourself with how examiners mark and assess real student responses
- Access interactive and alternative formats (e.g. videos, articles, podcasts) to suit your preferred learning styles

The following curated list includes high-quality websites, examiner materials, and revision platforms that extend beyond the basics. They are particularly useful for:

- High-achieving students looking to stretch their analysis
- Teachers seeking enrichment or discussion materials
- Anyone aiming to achieve a top grade through wider contextual understanding

Use these resources selectively and critically. Not all interpretations will align exactly with Edexcel's assessment criteria, but engaging with different viewpoints will strengthen your ability to form your own supported arguments.

ColourMyLearning

colourmylearning.com

For printable worksheets, revision summaries, and topic-by-topic blog posts, ColourMyLearning provides free, accessible content designed to complement this guide. Whether you're revising a theme, exploring character development, or practising PEEL writing, these articles reinforce your understanding and link directly to key exam skills.

New posts are added regularly to align with the Edexcel IGCSE and GCSE English Literature curriculum.

BBC Bitesize – An Inspector Calls (GCSE English Literature)

bbc.co.uk/bitesize

BBC Bitesize offers concise, reliable summaries of key characters, themes, and techniques for *An Inspector Calls*. Its visual layouts and quizzes make it especially useful for quick revision and consolidating understanding. While tailored for general GCSE, it complements the Edexcel IGCSE course effectively for foundational knowledge.

Edexcel Examiner Reports – English Literature Paper 2

qualifications.pearson.com

These official documents provide direct insight into how students are assessed in real exam conditions. Each report includes commentary on past responses, common mistakes, and advice from examiners. Essential reading for students aiming to refine their exam technique and understand how marks are awarded under AO1 and AO2.

Answer Key

Chapter 2 Story Overview

End of Chapter Self-test

Multiple Choice:

1. b. Brumley
2. c. 1912

Short Answer:

3. He sacked her for being one of the ringleaders in a strike demanding higher wages at his factory.
4. She had Eva dismissed out of jealousy and anger because Eva smiled at her while Sheila was trying on a dress.
5. A **cliffhanger**: the phone rings announcing a real inspector is on his way, echoing the earlier events and creating suspense.

Write Brief Notes:

6. **Write 3-4 bullet points summarising Gerald's involvement with Eva Smith/Daisy Renton:**

- Met her at the Palace Bar and helped her escape an unpleasant situation.
- Gave her a place to stay and supported her financially.
- Had an affair with her during the summer.
- Ended the relationship and left her, which contributed to her emotional downfall.

7. **What are two key ways the Inspector challenges the Birlings' worldview?**

- He promotes **collective responsibility**: "We are members of one body."
- He exposes the **moral failures of the upper class**, regardless of legality or status

Chapter 3 Main Characters

End of Chapter Self-test

Multiple Choice:

1. c. Sheila Birling Sheila represents moral growth, emotional awareness, and the hope for future change — a key figure in Priestley's vision of social reform.
2. b. Inspector Goole This line is part of the Inspector's final speech, reinforcing Priestley's theme of collective responsibility.

3. c. She is a symbolic figure who reveals others' moral failings Eva Smith, though silent, exposes the flaws of each character and represents the suffering of the working class.
4. b. "If you don't come down sharply on these people... Mr Birling's language shows his capitalist, authoritarian mindset and lack of social compassion.

Short Answer:

5. Sheila matures from a naïve and self-centred young woman to someone who fully accepts responsibility for her actions and challenges her family's moral failings.
6. Unlike his parents, Eric admits guilt and shows remorse. He accepts moral responsibility, while they remain defensive and focused on their reputation.
7. Sybil's reaction reveals deep class prejudice and a lack of empathy. She prioritises respectability and social hierarchy over compassion.
8. Gerald helps Eva temporarily and seems to care for her, but ultimately discards her and downplays the consequences. His failure to change shows his moral weakness.

Longer Tasks – Model Answer Outlines

9. **Character & Theme Connection**

Character: Inspector Goole

- **Summary:** The Inspector drives the plot by interrogating each character and revealing their moral failures.
- **Quotation:** *"We are members of one body."*
- **Analysis:** Priestley uses inclusive pronouns and emotive language to emphasise social responsibility. The Inspector acts as a moral force, representing Priestley's call for a fairer society.

10. **Compare & Contrast – Mr Birling vs Eric**

- **Attitudes:** Mr Birling is arrogant, dismissive, and never accepts blame; Eric is remorseful and acknowledges his wrongdoing.
- **Inspector's Impact:** Mr Birling deflects; Eric breaks down and changes.
- **Message:** Priestley contrasts generations to highlight the potential for future moral progress through the younger generation.

11. **Eva Smith's Symbolism**

- **How treated:** She is exploited, ignored, and discarded by each character.
- **Symbolic purpose:** She represents the working class, particularly voiceless women, and the consequences of a selfish society.
- **Significance of silence:** Eva never speaks on stage, which forces the audience to reconstruct her story and feel complicit in her suffering — a technique Priestley uses to prompt reflection and empathy.

Chapter 4 Context

End of Chapter Self-test

Multiple Choice:

1. **b. To highlight how little society had changed**
2. **c. World War II**
3. **c. Limited mobility and rigid structure**
4. **c. Advocacy for social responsibility**

Short Answer:

5. *They would likely have felt a sense of dramatic irony and frustration, recognising the foolish optimism of characters like Mr Birling who predict peace and progress.*
6. *As a democratic socialist, Priestley gives the Inspector moral authority to promote social responsibility, equality, and collective welfare.*
7. *Mr Birling makes bold statements (e.g., Titanic is unsinkable, no war will happen), which the audience knows to be false, undermining his credibility and symbolising flawed pre-war attitudes.*
8. *Eva's exploitation by different members of the upper and middle classes shows the vulnerability of working-class women with little social or legal protection.*

Longer Tasks – Context-Based Tasks (Sample Responses)

9. **Timeline of Events (1912-1945):**

   - 1912: The play's setting; Titanic sinks.
   - 1914-1918: World War I begins.
   - 1928: Women over 21 gain the vote in the UK.
   - 1939-1945: World War II.
   - 1945: Labour government elected, Beveridge Report and welfare reforms introduced.

10. **Paragraph - 1945 Audience Response:** A 1945 audience would likely view the Birlings critically, recognising their outdated views and moral failings. Having just come through a war that demanded national unity and sacrifice, audiences would be more receptive to Priestley's message of collective responsibility and the need to build a fairer, post-war society.

11. **Three Examples of Context Supporting AO2 Analysis:**

Mr Birling's speeches – His false optimism ("unsinkable", "no war") can be analysed as dramatic irony with political implications.

The Inspector – As Priestley's mouthpiece, his formal, didactic tone reflects the post-war push for social reform.

The cyclical ending – Suggests that history repeats unless society learns from its mistakes, reinforcing post-war urgency for change.

An Inspector Calls

Chapter 5 Main Themes and Key Quotes

End of Chapter Self-test

Multiple Choice:

1. c. Social Responsibility
2. b. Mrs Birling
3. b. Gerald's treatment of Eva
4. c. Moral Consequence
5. b. "Each of you helped to kill her."
6. c. "If you don't come down sharply on these people…"

Short Answer:

7. Priestley shows that younger characters like Sheila are open to learning and accepting responsibility, while older ones like Mr and Mrs Birling remain stubborn and dismissive, highlighting a conflict in values.
8. Eva represents the working class, constantly mistreated by those with power, showing how class status dictates opportunities and treatment in society.
9. Although he lacks social status, the Inspector holds moral authority. He challenges the Birlings' social power by questioning their ethics and exposing their failings.
10. Gerald appears honourable and respectable but hides his affair with Eva, revealing a gap between his public image and private behaviour.
11. Quote: "We all helped to kill her." This shows Eric's recognition of shared responsibility and emotional

maturity, contrasting with his earlier secrecy and recklessness.
12. Quotes like "I did nothing I'm ashamed of" and "Girls of that class—" show her moral detachment and prejudice, reinforcing Priestley's critique of the upper class.
13. Quote: "We are members of one body." The use of "we" promotes unity and shared moral responsibility, central to Priestley's socialist message.

Longer Tasks – Sample Responses

14. **Paragraph: Sheila and the Theme of Redemption**

Sheila's character arc illustrates the theme of redemption. At the start, she is superficial and unaware of her privilege, but upon learning of her role in Eva's dismissal, she expresses sincere remorse. Her willingness to reflect, change, and challenge others marks her as a character capable of moral growth. Through Sheila, Priestley suggests that acknowledging faults is the first step towards redemption and societal change.

15. Themes for Quotes

"But these girls aren't cheap labour – they're people." - Social Responsibility

"As if a girl of that sort would ever refuse money!" - Class Hierarchy

"Public men, Mr Birling, have responsibilities as well…" - Gender and Power

An Inspector Calls

Theme Paragraphs (sample answers)

16. Theme: Social Responsibility

The Inspector reflects the theme of social responsibility through his insistence that "we are members of one body." He encourages the characters to think beyond their individual interests and recognise the impact their actions have on others. Priestley uses the Inspector as a moral voice to show that real progress can only happen when people accept their duty to care for one another.

Theme: Gender and Power

Eva Smith's treatment reveals the vulnerability of women in Edwardian society. When Gerald describes her as "young and pretty and warm-hearted," it reflects how her value is reduced to appearance and gratitude. Priestley presents her experience as a critique of how gender and class combined to limit women's choices — and how men used power without consequence.

17. Statement Challenge

"Sheila learns more than any other character in the play." - Agree

Sheila begins as naive and self-centred but ends the play questioning her family's values and rejecting Gerald's proposal. Her line, "It frightens me the way you talk," shows her new awareness. Priestley uses her growth to represent the hope of a more responsible younger generation.

"Mr Birling cares more about reputation than people." – Agree

After the Inspector leaves, Mr Birling focuses on the risk of scandal rather than Eva's death. His concern that he "might have to appear before a public inquiry" shows that image matters more to him than ethics. Priestley uses Birling to criticise the selfish priorities of the upper class.

"The Inspector changes nothing." – Disagree

While the older generation resist change, the Inspector profoundly influences Sheila and Eric. Their acceptance of blame and moral growth suggests that his visit has a lasting effect. Priestley presents the Inspector as a force for reflection, even if not everyone listens.

"Eva Smith is the most powerful character in the play, despite never appearing." – Agree

Although she never speaks, Eva's story shapes the entire plot and exposes each character's flaws. The Inspector's line, "There are millions and millions of Eva Smiths," shows how she symbolises the forgotten and mistreated in society. Her absence makes her presence more powerful.

"Priestley believes that real change is only possible for the younger generation." - Partially agree

Sheila and Eric accept responsibility, showing they are open to change. However, the ending — with the second phone call — leaves the possibility open that others might also change under the right circumstances. Priestley seems to place hope in youth, but still warns that everyone must be willing to learn.

Chapter 6 Glossary of Literary and Dramatic Terms

End of Chapter Self-test

Multiple Choice:

1. b. The audience knowing more than the characters
2. c. Cyclical structure
3. c. Hints or clues about future events

Short Answer:

4. **Stage directions** are instructions in the script that describe movement, setting, or tone, while **dialogue** is the spoken interaction between characters.
5. An example of **symbolism** is the **Inspector** in *An Inspector Calls*, who symbolises collective conscience and moral authority.
6. **Subtext** reveals characters' unspoken thoughts or motivations, helping the audience understand emotional tension and hidden meaning.

Fill in the Blanks

7. motif
8. monologue
9. contrast

Reflection Prompt *(Example Response)*

10. *Dramatic irony, symbolism,* and *stage directions* help me explore how the playwright creates meaning. I use them to show how characters are exposed, how key ideas are reinforced, and how the audience is guided through emotional responses.

Chapter 7 Language Form and Structure

End of Chapter Self-test

Multiple Choice:

1. **b. It highlights his ignorance** Dramatic irony undermines Mr Birling's authority by showing the audience that his confident statements (e.g. about war and the Titanic) are wrong.
2. **c. It increases moral and emotional pressure** The single setting of the dining room creates a claustrophobic atmosphere, enhancing the intensity of the Inspector's interrogation.

Short Answer:

3. **Example Answer:** *"She died in misery and agony – hating life."* This is emotive language used by the Inspector to generate sympathy for Eva and highlight the severity of the Birlings' actions.
4. A cyclical structure means the play ends in a similar way to how it began. Priestley uses this by having a second phone call at the end, suggesting the events may repeat themselves. This reinforces the theme of

An Inspector Calls

learning from mistakes and the consequences of inaction.

Explain & Explore:

5. **Example Answers:** The younger generation (Sheila and Eric) show guilt and willingness to change, while the older generation (Mr and Mrs Birling) deny responsibility. This contrast supports Priestley's belief in social reform through younger, more open-minded individuals.

OR

The older generation (Mr and Mrs Birling) refuse to accept responsibility, showing stubbornness and denial. In contrast, the younger generation (Sheila and Eric) show remorse and a willingness to change. Priestley uses this to suggest hope for a more socially responsible future lies with the youth.

6. **Example Answers:** One key structural feature is the sequential revelations. Each character's involvement with Eva is revealed one by one, which builds dramatic tension and emphasises the cumulative moral failure of the entire group.

OR

Feature: Cliffhanger ending.

Effect: The sudden final phone call disrupts the family's sense of relief and forces the audience to consider whether they will learn from their mistakes. It keeps the play's moral message unresolved, encouraging reflection.

Chapter 9 Quick Recap Tools

Fill-in-the-Blanks – Key Quotes

1. "We are members of one **body**."
2. "The **time** is not the important thing. It's what happened to the girl and what we all did to her that matters."
3. "There are millions and millions of Eva Smiths and **John** Smiths still left with us."
4. "But these girls aren't cheap **labour** – they're people."
5. "She was a lively good-looking girl – country-bred, I fancy – and she'd had a lot to say – far too much – so she had to go." (Who said this? **Mr Birling**)
6. "I suppose we're all nice people now." (Spoken by: **Sheila Birling**)

Final Multiple Choice Questions

7. b. Responsibility and change
8. b. Dramatic irony
9. a. Forgiveness
10. c. Delivers Priestley's moral message
11. b. Cyclical

Final Writing Practice – Sample PETAL Paragraph

Sample Answer:

Priestley uses Eric to show how younger people are more open to change than the older generation. When Eric says, "You're not the kind of father a chap could go to when he's in trouble," the use of direct address and emotional tone reveals the lack of trust between Eric and Mr Birling. This shows a breakdown in communication and highlights the failure of traditional authority figures. Priestley uses Eric to represent a generation that questions outdated values and is willing to accept responsibility. Through Eric's development, Priestley encourages the audience to place hope in younger voices for a more compassionate future.

Acknowledgments

Thank you to the students, teachers, and tutors who have inspired the development of this guide — especially those who ask thoughtful questions, think deeply about the text, and remind us that good literature invites reflection as well as analysis.

Special thanks to everyone who helped review and refine this material, ensuring that it remains both rigorous and accessible. Your feedback has made this guide clearer, stronger, and more useful to students preparing for real exams under real pressure.

Finally, to every reader working through this book — whether you're revising late at night, learning in class, or working hard to build confidence in your own time — thank you. This guide was written for you.

Also by Colour My Learning

Looking for revision guides for other texts?

Explore our full collection of study resources, including upcoming titles, past paper questions, and blog support, at:

www.colourmylearning.com/revision

Whether you're studying *Macbeth*, *Of Mice and Men*, *Jekyll & Hyde*, or poetry, you'll find updates, free materials, and downloadable tools to help you prepare.

Stay up to date and check what's new — we're constantly adding more.

www.ingramcontent.com/pod-product-compliance
Lightning Source LLC
Chambersburg PA
CBHW052052070526
44584CB00017B/2139